The Trauma
of Everyday Life

ALSO BY MARK EPSTEIN:

Thoughts without a Thinker:
Psychotherapy from a Buddhist Perspective

Going to Pieces without Falling Apart:
A Buddhist Perspective on Wholeness

Going on Being:
Buddhism and the Way of Change

Open to Desire:
The Truth About What the Buddha Taught

Psychotherapy without the Self:
A Buddhist Perspective

The Trauma
of Everyday Life

MARK EPSTEIN, MD

THE PENGUIN PRESS
New York
2013

THE PENGUIN PRESS
Published by the Penguin Group
Penguin Group (USA) Inc., 375 Hudson Street,
New York, New York 10014, USA

USA · Canada · UK · Ireland · Australia
New Zealand · India · South Africa · China

Penguin Books Ltd, Registered Offices: 80 Strand, London WC2R 0RL, England
For more information about the Penguin Group visit penguin.com

A portion of Chapter Six first appeared on the "Goop" website, January 13, 2010.

Grateful acknowledgment is made for permission to reprint the following copyrighted works:
Excerpt from *The Notebooks of Malte Laurids Briggs* by Rainer Maria Rilke, translated by
Michael Hulse (Penguin Classics, 2009). Translation copyright © Michael Hulse, 2009.
Reprinted by permission of Penguin Books Ltd.
"The Tree" by D. W. Winnicott. By permission of The Marsh Agency Ltd
on behalf of The Winnicott Trust.

Library of Congress Cataloging-in-Publication Data
Epstein, Mark, 1953–
The trauma of everyday life / Mark Epstein, MD.
pages cm
Includes bibliographical references and index.
ISBN 978-1-59420-513-2
1. Psychic trauma.   2. Life change events—Psychological aspects.   3. Stress
(Psychology)   4. Interpersonal relations.   I. Title.
RC552.T7E67 2013
616.85'21—dc23
2013007698

Printed in the United States of America
3   5   7   9   10   8   6   4   2

Book design by Amanda Dewey

AUTHOR'S NOTE

Except in the case of well-known figures introduced by first and last names, I have changed names and other identifying details or constructed composites in order to protect privacy.

To Arlene

Contents

Only one step, and my deep misery would be beatitude.

—Rainer Maria Rilke,
The Notebooks of Malte Laurids Brigge

1

The Way Out Is Through

For the first ten years of my work as a psychiatrist, I did not think much about trauma. I was in my thirties, and many of the people I worked with were not much older than I was. In the first flush of my marriage, most of my efforts were directed toward helping my patients find and achieve the kind of love and intimacy they wanted and deserved. In retrospect, I should have been alerted to the ubiquity of trauma by the fact that three of the first patients I ever cared for were young women on an inpatient psychiatric ward who each attempted suicide after breaking up with their boyfriends. Their experiences were all similar. The stability and security they were counting on suddenly vanished. The earth moved and their worlds collapsed. While I helped them to recover, it took me many more years to understand that their reactions were far from unique. They were impulsive, young, vulnerable, and full of unrealistic expectations, but they were being forced to deal with an uncomfortable truth that we all have to face in one form or another. Trauma is an indivisible part of human existence. It takes many forms but spares no one.

Ten years into my therapy practice, three women in their early thirties came to see me within three months of one another. Each of their husbands had dropped dead. One left in the morning to ride his mountain bike and had a heart attack, one lay stricken on the tennis court, and one did not wake up in the morning. Each of these women's losses challenged my therapeutic approach. They had already found the love and intimacy I was endeavoring to help my patients achieve. They needed something else from me.

Around this same time, one of my long-term patients, a man about my own age, received a frightening diagnosis. He had a condition that threatened his life but that was known to have a highly variable course, discovered in a routine blood test. He might be severely sick soon, with a bone marrow cancer called multiple myeloma, or he might be fine for a long while. Only time, and careful monitoring, would tell. When he first told me, I reacted with genuine concern and barely disguised horror. He responded to my concern with alarm.

"I don't need sympathy from you," he said. "I can get that from other people. I need something different from you. This diagnosis is a fact, is it not? I can't treat it like a tragedy. That's why I'm coming to you. I know you understand that."

My patient's comment brought me up short. I knew he was right. His condition was mirroring the breakups, losses, and deaths that had been knocking at my door. His query, "This illness is a fact, is it not?" rang in my ears. What could I offer him? Already deeply influenced by the philosophy and psychology of Buddhism, I turned to it again for help. What I found did not really surprise me—in some sense I knew it already—but it helped me, and my patient, a great deal. In its most succinct form, it was what the Buddha called Realistic View. In the prescription for the end of suffering that he outlined in his Four Noble Truths, Realistic View held an important place. A critical component of what became known as the Noble Eightfold Path, Realistic View counseled that trauma, in any of its forms, is not a failure or a mistake.

It is not something to be ashamed of, not a sign of weakness, and not a reflection of inner failing. It is simply a fact of life.

This attitude toward trauma is at the heart of the Buddha's teaching, although it is often overlooked in the rush to embrace the inner peace that his teachings also promised. But inner peace is actually predicated upon a realistic approach to the uncertainties and fears that pervade our lives. Western psychology often teaches that if we understand the cause of a given trauma we can move past it, returning to the steady state we imagine is normal. Many who are drawn to Eastern practices hope that they can achieve their own steady state. They use religious techniques to quiet their minds in the hope of rising above the intolerable feelings that life evokes. Both strategies, at their core, seek to escape from trauma, once and for all. But trauma is all pervasive. It does not go away. It continues to reassert itself as life unfolds. The Buddha taught that a realistic view makes all the difference. If one can treat trauma as a fact and not as a failing, one has the chance to learn from the inevitable slings and arrows that come one's way. Meditation makes profound use of this philosophy, but its utility is not limited to meditation. As my patient realized when grappling with his diagnosis, the traumas of everyday life, if they do not destroy us, become bearable, even illuminating, when we learn to relate to them differently.

When I first came upon the Buddha's teachings, I was young and not really thinking about illness or death. No one I knew had died, and I was struggling with my own issues of adolescence and young adulthood. Trauma, in the sense of confronting an actual or threatened death or serious injury (as the American Psychiatric Association's *Diagnostic and Statistical Manual of Mental Disorders* defines "trauma"), was not something I had to face directly. But there was another kind of trauma, developmental trauma, percolating under the surface of my experience. Developmental trauma occurs when "emotional pain cannot find a relational home in which it can be held."[1] In retrospect, I can see that this was the case for me. In my first encounters with Buddhism, I was trying to escape from emotional pain I did not really understand. But in order to practice the Buddha's teachings, I needed a realistic view. This meant accepting there was no escape. The most important spiritual experiences of my early exploration of Buddhism gave me such a view, although I have had to be reminded of it time and again as circumstances have evolved. This is what I remembered in response to my patient's plea, however. What I learned in grappling with my own trauma was relevant in his struggle, too.

I could tell, when I first came upon Buddhism, that there was going to be a problem getting it right. There were too many paradoxes for there not to be. Self appears but does not truly exist, taught the Buddha. Change your thoughts but remain as you are, said the Dalai Lama. The mind that does not understand is the Buddha; there is no other, wrote the Zen philosopher D. T. Suzuki. I was excited by these teachings—they rang true in some ill-defined way—but it was not easy to make the transition from conceptual appreciation to experiential understanding. Nor could I even say with confidence that I truly understood things conceptually. At the time of my introduction to Buddhism, I was still a college student and I was good at only one thing: studying. I knew how to write a paper, prepare for a test, gather information, and analyze it a little bit. I had figured out how to be reasonably comfortable in an academic environment, but I was after something more, although I found it difficult to put my finger on just what that might be.

Whenever I tried to put it into words it sounded banal. While comfortable in my academic world, I was uncomfortable with myself. Deep down, I felt unsure. Not of my intellectual skills but of something more amorphous. I could frame it in terms of existential anxiety or even adolescent ennui, but it felt more personal than that. I worried there was something wrong with me, and I longed to feel more at ease. I had the sense that I was living on the surface of myself, that I was keeping myself more two-dimensional than I really was, that I was inhibited, or was inhibiting myself, in some ill-defined way. I felt boring, although I framed it in terms of feeling empty. To admit that I felt boring would have made me feel too ashamed.

Buddhism appealed to me because, while it hinged on paradox, it also seemed very logical. It spoke directly to my feelings of anxiety and even promised that there was something concrete to do about them. The Buddha, in his First Noble Truth, affirmed my experience by invoking *dukkha*, or suffering, as a basic fact of life. He spoke about it very psychologically; he even specified that there was something uncomfortable about the self in particular, some way that it could not help but disappoint. This made me feel relieved, as if to suggest that I was not making it up. If the Buddha had noticed it all those years ago, maybe it was not just *my* problem; maybe there was even something to do about it.

The first words of the Buddha that I ever read, preserved in a collection called the *Dhammapada*, reinforced my feeling of hopefulness by speaking directly to my helplessness. He seemed to be describing my own mind.

> Flapping like a fish thrown on dry ground,
> it trembles all day, struggling.

I liked the image of the fish on dry ground. It spoke of my discomfort, of what I would now call a feeling of estrangement, a sense of not being at peace, or at one, with myself. And it caught the feeling of my anxiety perfectly. But there was more than just a diagnosis of the problem in the Buddha's approach. There was a science to it that I found reassuring, an inner science.

> Like an archer an arrow,
> the wise man steadies his trembling mind,
> a fickle and restless weapon.

The Buddha had a solution, something to do for the problem, a way of working directly with the mind that appealed to the budding therapist in me. There was a path with a goal and a concrete method that one could practice in order to feel better.

> The mind is restless.
> To control it is good.
> A disciplined mind is the road to Nirvana.[2]

I was excited by the promise of the Buddha's psychology, drawn to it before ever learning much about Western therapy. I could see that my mind needed work, and the Buddha's prescription of self-investigation and mental discipline, what he called "mindfulness and clear comprehension," made intuitive sense to me. Yet the more I learned about meditation the clearer it became that there was a limit to how far I could think, or reason, or even practice my way in. I wanted to understand and master it, but it frustrated me when I approached it. Whenever I sat down to meditate, my own insecurities rose to the surface. I was never sure if I was doing it *right*.

I have written of how my first understanding of meditation came from learning to juggle. I was at a Buddhist summer institute in Colorado in the summer after my junior year in college. The faculty was full of Buddhist teachers: university professors, Tibetan lamas, Zen *roshis*,

American Peace Corps veterans in the process of becoming meditation teachers. I took classes from all of them, but my roommates, randomly assigned to me for the summer months, stopped going to class after a week or two, turned off by the pretension of many of the most popular instructors. They watched me laboring at meditation and after some time took pity on me. One day, they offered to teach me to juggle.

I was up for the challenge and worked at it assiduously. After several days of practice, I succeeded at keeping three balls in the air. My mind relaxed and I momentarily stopped worrying about keeping everything together. A new kind of space opened up in which everything flowed in its own way and I settled into it. I was present but not in the way, attentive and physically active but not interfering, detached but not disinterested, watching but at the same time completely involved. My familiar and troubled self did not disappear; it became one more thing to be aware of, one of the balls I was juggling. Instead of secretly fighting with it in the back of my mind, I became more accepting of my troubling inner feelings. I sensed a shift in my basic orientation to life, an easing of my self-centeredness, more of an ability to take myself lightly.

I also found that it was possible to maintain this new frame of mind, both when I was juggling and, sometimes, when I was not. If I kept a light and steady touch on my mind, something of the juggling remained with me. If I tried too hard, thought about it too much, or, conversely, relaxed altogether, the balls fell out of the air. But if I dropped all that and just juggled, it seemed to take care of itself. Juggling and, by implication, meditation required that I suspend my usual orientation and enter some new territory, an intermediate zone that seemed to create something new or evoke something old. My hands were not only juggling the balls; they were juggling my mind. Or maybe my mind was doing the juggling, not my hands. And where was "I," the troubled and anxious "me," the one who was worried about being good enough, in this process? I really could not say. Intrigued and, for the moment, relieved, I returned to my meditation classes. I had a new way to approach meditation now, and a new orientation to myself.

I began to appreciate that Buddhism demanded something more of me than studying and also something more than just rote practice. Not that it did not engage my intellect—it did. And not that it did not encourage conceptual rigor and rigorous effort—these were things I appreciated about it. But it demanded something in addition. I knew nothing of art at this time, but I can see now that Buddhism is as much inner art as it is inner science. It is a formless art, to be sure—the only product is the self, and even *that* comes quickly into continuous question—but it is an art nonetheless, one that demands its own touch, one I could only understand to the extent that I could give myself over to it completely. This emphasis on surrender and process was not one that I knew before I came upon Buddhism—perhaps if I had been a musician or an actor or a painter or a poet, it would not have seemed like such a revelation—but for me it was like stumbling into a new reality, one in which I was suddenly being asked to give of myself in a new way. In Zen, the image of falling backward into a well is used to describe what it is like. For me it was like feeling my way into myself while blindfolded, never quite sure what I would find.

Feeling my way into myself. That was definitely what it was like. Feeling my way into all of the doubts and anxieties and insecurities and dis-ease that I would have been all too happy to get rid of, that I had initially hoped meditation would destroy. Feeling my way into them, in my body as well as in my mind, and feeling my way through them. Something changed as I embraced the art of meditation. Instead of approaching myself with dread, with the secret hope that I could rise above my personal struggles, I began to explore the texture of my own suffering. No one had ever told me such a thing was possible. Even as I practiced under the tutelage of a new generation of Buddhist teachers, I had trouble reconciling my experience with what I was learning from my Buddhist books. The fundamental psychological teaching of the Buddha was called *anatman* (in Sanskrit) or *anatta* (in Pali, the language of the Buddhist scriptures, a Sanskrit-related tongue closer to what the Buddha must have spoken), meaning no-soul or no-self. My Buddhist teachers stressed this at every opportunity. Part of my initial attraction to Buddhism lay in this central concept. I liked that there was an alternative to the Western preoccupation with self, to the psychoanalytic effort to build up the ego. "Where *id* was, there *ego* shall be," pronounced Freud in a famous maxim that I had already unconsciously subscribed to. Not quite ready to relinquish my id (still in the process of finding it, in fact), I liked the counterintuitive implications of no-self, the allure of egolessness. I liked the very sound of it. It took away some kind of pressure I had been feeling to make myself into someone I could put my finger on, something I could explain. It let me off the hook a little, relaxed me, gave me a sense of relief. No self. It had a nice ring. While most other people were busy making themselves bigger, better, and stronger, I could head in a different direction. Go to zero. Less is more, wasn't that what people were saying? Maybe I could leave my id alone after all.

But my understanding of no-self was limited at this point. I took it to mean that my inner anxiety, my "self," was unreal and would drop away once I woke up. It was confusing to find that meditation—rather than dropping me into a void of no-self—backed me into myself. It tricked me, so to speak. The paradox that lured me to Buddhism in the beginning did not resolve as I became more familiar with the Buddha's words; it deepened. While meditation was teaching me to hold myself with a light touch, it was also helping me to emerge, to emerge *through* my suffering, not in spite of it. I continued to study Buddhist theory, of course, and I understood, theoretically, that there was no self to be found, that what we took for a self was only a conglomeration of parts, just as a car is made up of wheels, axles, motors, chassis, and so forth. In the Buddhist sutras, the Buddha called the parts that are construed in their interaction as a self the five *skandhas*, the five "heaps" or "aggregates." Form, feelings, perceptions, mental processes, and consciousness were the five *skandhas*; I knew that. There was no self; there were only the aggregates. That was one of the fundamental principles of the Buddhist path, repeated at the outset of every teaching. Yet the more experience I had with meditation, the more connected I felt with myself. Where before I had been living on the surface, secretly afraid that I was missing something or that there was something off about me, I now felt—how else can I phrase it?—more at home. Instead of dropping away permanently, as I, newly schooled in Buddhist metaphysics, hoped and expected it would do, my self seemed to be broadening its horizons.

Affirmation that I might not be completely off base came to me from the Buddhist sutras themselves. In one, there is a story about a conversation between the Buddha and the king of Kosala, one of the kingdoms where the Buddha roamed. Why is it that your followers seem so different from those of other teachers and sects? this king wanted to know. You emphasize the inescapability of *dukkha*, the truth of suffering, and yet your monks look so full of life. The followers of other religions look "haggard, coarse, pale, emaciated, and unprepossessing," the king went on, while your disciples are "joyful, elated, jubilant, and exultant." They even seem "light-hearted," the king continued, as if they have "a gazelle's mind."[3] This was indeed a strange religion. How was it that a willingness to embrace suffering yielded such a sense of vitality?

The king was seeing what I was feeling. The fruits of meditation— balance, ease, joyfulness, and humor—seemed to emerge in conjunction with an acknowledgment of suffering. This was strange, I thought. But I could not ignore the shift that was taking place inside of me. While Buddhism taught about no-self, my own experience was to feel more connected, more alive, less at odds with or afraid of myself, and more able to rest in my own consciousness. I was less fraught, less worried about the state of myself, less preoccupied with what was wrong with me and more able to just be. The feelings of being like a fish out of water were beginning to diminish.

I have come to realize that this paradoxical strategy was one of the Buddha's greatest discoveries. Trauma happens to everyone. The potential for it is part of the precariousness of human existence. Some traumas—loss, death, accidents, disease, and abuse—are explicit; others—like the emotional deprivation of an unloved child—are more subtle; and some, like my own feelings of estrangement, seem to come from nowhere. But it is hard to imagine the scope of an individual life without envisioning some kind of trauma, and it is hard for most people to know what to do about it. I remember talking to my father just before he died from a malignant brain tumor a couple of years ago. He was eighty-four years old, an accomplished physician who had lived a long and productive life and had worked steadily until his tumor was discovered a month or so earlier, too late for treatment.

"Have you made your peace with what is happening?" I asked him somewhat awkwardly in one of our final conversations, tiptoeing around the dreaded word "death."

"I could say that I'm trying," he said, his words coming slowly and haltingly now. "But I feel like I'm finally up against something I can't do anything about."

It is rare for someone to get through life without facing trauma. I know my father had his share—at fifteen he injected his own father with morphine as he lay dying of mesothelioma, an asbestos-caused lung cancer he came down with after insulating his own attic—but I think he did his best to keep it out of his consciousness for as long as he could. The Buddha counseled another way. He saw the mind and the heart as one and he used a rather strange phrase to talk about how a realistic view of trauma helps people. It "gladdens their hearts," he said on many occasions. The king of Kosala noticed it in his time and I noticed it in mine but it was not the conventional approach in his era and it is certainly not the standard in ours.

The Buddha was not a physician, although he was often described as one, at least partly because he gave his first set of teachings, on the Four Noble Truths, in the form traditionally used by doctors of his time to present their cases.[4] Like them, he described the illness, gave its cause, declared that a cure was available, and laid out the components of the treatment. In so doing, he pushed against the constraints of his culture. An ancient Sanskrit proverb declares, "One should not speak unless what one says is both true and pleasant."[5] Buddha rejected this view. There was nothing pleasant about his First Noble Truth, spoken by him in the form of a one-word exclamation: "*Dukkha!*" The word, generally translated as "suffering" but carrying the literal meaning of "hard to face," was the Buddha's emphatic summary of the entire human predicament. When forced to elaborate on what he meant, the Buddha let loose with a torrent of explanation. Birth, aging, sickness, death, sorrow, lamentation, pain, grief, and despair are inescapable; being close to those who are disagreeable, being separated from those who are loved, and not getting what one wants are all unpleasant facts of life; indeed, just being a person in this world brings suffering because of how insignificant we feel and how impermanent we are. Even pleasant experiences carry a whiff of dissatisfaction because of their inability to provide ultimate comfort. No matter how fulfilling, they eventually run their course.

But there was another quality to the *dukkha* the Buddha described, a more subtle description of the unsatisfactory nature of the human predicament. The word itself is a compound with an interesting derivation. The prefix "duh" means badness or difficulty, while the suffix "kha" can refer to the hole at the center of a wheel into which an axle fits. The word thus connotes a bad fit making for a bumpy ride.[6] For me this image of a poorly fitting axle was another way of describing the sense of not fitting in, of not quite belonging, of being slightly at odds with oneself, that had afflicted me for as long as I could remember. It was probably no accident, given the derivation of the word, that the Buddha's teaching of the Four Noble Truths was entitled "Setting in Motion the Wheel of the Dharma." His listeners would have been aware of the connotations of the word *dukkha* and would have appreciated the imagery of the Buddha turning a wheel smoothly.

Questioned some years after his enlightenment by a local prince about his penchant for delivering bad news, Buddha said that he could no longer abide by the traditional Sanskrit principle of saying only what was true and pleasant. He marched to a different drum, he maintained, and would speak of what was "true and beneficial even if it was disagreeable." To illustrate his point, he pointed to a baby on the prince's lap. What if the infant put a stick or a pebble in his mouth? Wouldn't the prince pull it out even if doing so were likely to cause the baby some distress? Wasn't that what a doctor sometimes had to do? Not to mention a mother? But he added one caveat. He would speak the beneficial, if disagreeable, truth only if he "knew the time to say it."[7] As is the case with good therapists today, tact was a major concern of the Buddha. If someone was not ready to acknowledge his or her trauma, he would not force the issue. Each individual had to liberate him- or herself, after all. The best a teacher, even a Buddha, can do is to show them how.

"This generation is entangled in a tangle," began one of the earliest commentaries on the Buddha's teachings, written many generations ago in Sri Lanka, somewhere around the fifth century of the common era. The "tangle" refers to the way we only want to hear what is "true and pleasant," the way we refuse what is "disagreeable." In the Buddha's time as well as in our own, there was a rush toward some imagined version of normal, an intolerance of the precarious foundation upon which we are perched. It was true thousands of years ago and it remains true to this day. The novelist William Styron once expressed this perfectly. Overheard when he was a young man in Paris drunkenly falling into his oysters and pleading to his friends for relief, Styron gave voice to what for most people remains an unacknowledged whisper in the back of their minds. "Ah ain' got no mo reesistunce to change than a *snow*-flake," Styron moaned. "Ah'm goin' home to the James Rivuh and grow *pee*-nuts."[8] Styron's willingness to acknowledge his trauma is unusual—most of us refuse to admit it, even to ourselves, but live in a state of entanglement with it nonetheless.

A patient of mine recently gave voice to a similar sentiment in the midst of her therapy with me. She was sober, and she had a different image for her suffering, but she was pleading in much the same way as William Styron: "I feel like a person alone in a sailboat in the middle of the ocean clinging for dear life to the mast," Monica confided as she began to well up, the silence of her therapy session cushioning her tears. "It's too much; I can't hang on any longer; I don't know what else to do." An accomplished and beloved professor in her midfifties, Monica was astute enough to be able to give language to her trauma, one that many people feel but shy away from. She, too, was like a fish out of water. There was an urgency to her communication, I remember, a desperation, but also an honesty. I think it came in the context of talking about her mother's declining health, but I recognized the feeling and did not think it was only about her mother's impending demise. I was too familiar with what she was talking about to attribute it solely to the approaching loss of her mom.

Life's difficulties often reduce us to the feeling Monica was talking about, I thought. What with war and earthquakes and rape and disease, it's a wonder life is not more difficult more of the time. But even if we push natural or man-made disasters to one side and try to stick to normal everyday life, things are still a struggle. Life is beautiful sometimes, for sure; in fact, it's totally amazing, every day a good day; but that doesn't stop things from being fragile and precarious, nor does it stop us from feeling all too alone. Of course, the line between normal everyday life and calamity seems extraordinarily thin sometimes, but regular life, even in its glory, is difficult. Things don't always go the way they should. Our friends and loved ones struggle. The specter of loss is always hovering. And we often feel adrift, unmoored, fearful, and out of our depth.

Luckily, I did not relay any of these thoughts to Monica. Something more vital popped out of my mouth.

"But you're the ocean, as well," I replied.

Several years later, after her mother had passed away, Monica reminded me of my comment. It had had a tremendous impact, she said. I was surprised—I could have just as easily made a case for her *not* being the ocean—but I was glad I had been able to say something that mattered, something she remembered, something that made her think. So much of therapy happens in the moment and passes right out of memory. There was a Buddhist slant to my retort, I reflected. It hit on something I had learned from my own experience. Trauma is the way into the self, and the way out. To be free, to come to terms with our lives, we have to have a direct experience of ourselves as we really are, warts and all. To understand selflessness—the central and liberating concept I was reaching for when I reminded Monica of her oceanic nature—we have to first find the self that we take to be so real, the one that is pushing us around in life, the one that feels traumatized, entangled in a tangle. The freedom the Buddha envisioned does not come from jettisoning imprisoning thoughts and feelings or from abandoning the suffering self; it comes from learning how to hold it all differently, juggling them rather than cleaving to their ultimate realities.

Monica was at a pivotal point in therapy, a pivotal point in her life. Some might say she was regressed, but there is an inherent prejudice in this word that connotes an almost universal fear of the emergence of such strong feelings of dread. Monica was in touch with herself on a primitive level, and this was a real accomplishment. She really did feel alone, adrift, and afraid. However much I might have wanted to comfort her, to show her how her current feelings were conditioned by early childhood experiences of deprivation and were therefore presently unreal, I restrained myself. From my perspective, her willingness to expose her true feelings was a great opportunity. On one level, Monica was in touch with her reality. There she was, clutching the mast of her identity. On another level, she was poised for a breakthrough. All around her, just outside her apprehension, was the liberating ocean of her mind.

I was reaching for this when I was speaking with Monica. I was not thinking of Freud's oceanic feeling, of the way Freud reduced spiritual experience to a resurrection of infantile oneness with the mother at the breast. I was not trying to tell her that she and her mom were one despite her mother's impending death, and I was not trying to show her the childhood or infantile origins of her painful feelings: I was indicating to her that she was actually one step away from understanding her true nature. Her conviction about her predicament was inadvertently summoning an image of its release. Convinced that she was clinging to the mast of her ship, she was nonetheless painting a picture of the sea. And somewhere inside, when I pointed out the huge part of her internal landscape she was ignoring, Monica let go, just a little.

This rhythm, of trauma and its release, is one that runs through Buddhism like a great underground river. I say underground because, even within Buddhist culture, it is not always clearly acknowledged.

There is a hidden trauma at the heart of the Buddha's own story, for example, one that is known but not often spoken of, one that I have found full of meaning despite the lack of attention it has garnered over the years. The Buddha's mother died seven days after giving birth to him. Overtly, in the myths and legends that have grown up around the life of the Buddha, very little is made of this fact. But scratch the surface of the Buddha's biography and you can see a metaphor churning away, lying in wait, one might say, for the psychologically minded times we are now living in. Something was nagging at the Buddha's heart, something he had no memory of, a taste of suffering so early in his life that, for all intents and purposes, it should not have mattered. Raised by loving parents—his mother's sister stepped in and took care of him like her own—and surrounded by all the joy and wealth and caring attention his parents could muster, the young man who was to become the Buddha nevertheless felt that something was wrong. Whether this feeling stemmed from the loss of his biological mother or from a later confrontation with the realities of old age, sickness, and death we do not know, but the presence of this early loss in his psyche creates a motif that anyone who struggles with inexplicable feelings of estrangement or alienation can relate to. The traumas of everyday life can easily make us feel like a motherless child.

In responding to Monica, I was making a critical point. It is not as important to find the *cause* of our traumatized feelings as it is to learn how to relate to them. Because everyday life is so challenging, there is a great need to pretend. Our most intimate feelings get shunted to the side, relegated to our dreams. We all want to be normal. Life, even normal life, is arduous, demanding, and ultimately threatening. We all have to deal with it, and none of us really knows how. We are all traumatized by life, by its unpredictability, its randomness, its lack of regard for our feelings and the losses it brings. Each in our own way, we suffer. Even if nothing else goes wrong (and it is rare that this is the case), old age, illness, and death loom just over the horizon, like the monsters our children need us to protect them from in the night.

The story of the Buddha's enlightenment shows him confronting his own trauma and using it to broaden the horizons of his mind. A Buddhist teacher of mine, whom I met years ago in Boulder in my initial explorations of Buddhism, has a pithy way of describing how the Buddha accomplished this. When dealing with painful emotions, Joseph Goldstein (now a respected American Buddhist and the cofounder of the Insight Meditation Society in Barre, Massachusetts) suggests, *the way out is through*. Emotional pain is as fruitful an object of awareness as anything else; it may even have qualities, like intensity, that make it particularly useful as a means of training the mind. In exploring the Buddha's life story, we can see him doing just this. He may not have known where his feelings of trauma came from, but he was able to create for himself the inner environment of attunement and responsiveness that he needed. His success is a model for the rest of us. Confronted with unpleasant feelings that we often are at a loss to explain, we can learn to use those feelings to show us the oceans of our minds.

In a famous statement, the Buddha once said that he "taught one thing. Suffering and its end." As has often been pointed out, to most ears this sounds like two things.[9] But the Buddha was choosing his words carefully. The clear-eyed comprehension of suffering permits its release. The Buddha, in his role as therapist, showed how this was possible. The great promise of his teachings was that suffering is only the First Truth and that acknowledging it opens up the others. By the time the Buddha, turning the wheel of the dharma, got to the Third Truth and the Fourth Truth (the End of Suffering and the Eightfold Path to its Relief), he had filled his listeners with new hope. Trauma, he was saying, while an indisputable fact of life, did not have to be the last word.

2

Primitive Agony

I t took the Buddha six years of self-imposed exile to find his way out of suffering and some extra time after his awakening to organize his insights into the Four Noble Truths. At first, postenlightenment, he was a bit tongue-tied. It is said that in the immediate aftermath of his nirvana, he was convinced that no one would be able to understand him. "This world is anguished," he affirmed to himself, "and even that which we call self is ill. No one will ever see what goes against the stream, is subtle, abstruse, deep and hard to see."[1] People were too entangled in their tangles to open in the way he now knew was possible. Trying to articulate his expansive vision in the face of their disbelief would be tiresome, he thought to himself; it would be wearying and troublesome. "I saw vexation in the telling,"[2] the Buddha reminisced later, and he relented, it is said, only after the pleading of Brahma, highest of the gods, who implored him that there were a handful of people "with little dust on their eyes" who would be grateful for the chance to hear his teachings.

Still, the Buddha was not immediately successful in articulating himself. He scoured the universe with his divine eye after Brahma's intervention, searching for the two major teachers of his preawakening years. They had shown him how to control his mind, although they had not been able to free him completely from his pain. They were wise, learned, and discerning, the Buddha thought. They had little dust on their eyes. They would be ones who could soon understand him. But, as if to accentuate the unpredictable nature of reality, the Buddha saw that both men had recently died. One had passed away the week before and one the previous evening. At a loss, the Buddha set out to find five old friends he had recently spent time with in the forest doing self-punishing spiritual practice. On the way, the first person he encountered was another acquaintance from his days as a forest ascetic, a wandering Ajivka named Upaka. Upaka was immediately impressed with the Buddha's radiant complexion but was suspicious of his claims of enlightenment.

"Your faculties are serene, friend; the color of your skin is clear and bright! Who is your teacher?" the friend exclaimed. The Buddha responded with a long description of his accomplishments, proclaiming that he had no teacher, had freed himself by virtue of his own wisdom, and had peered deeply into the blissful nature of reality. He challenged Upaka's ascetic worldview right from the start by affirming that nirvana was present in the here and now and not dependent on self-mortification.

"I am an All-transcender, an All-knower," he explained. "In a blindfold world I go to beat the Deathless Drum."[3]

Upaka would have none of it and shrugged the Buddha off, unimpressed with his poetry. Deeply immersed in the prevailing ideology of his time, Upaka believed that painful experiences needed to be accentuated in order to yield their purifying effects. Everyday life was not nearly traumatic enough for him; he was out for something much more punishing. He had known the Buddha when both of them were engaged in torturing themselves as a spiritual pursuit. By subjecting themselves to extremes of hunger, thirst, pain, and physical discomfort, ascetics of their time hoped to liberate their spirits from the prisons of their flesh. To see the Buddha looking so healthy was one big shock—to hear him describing the blissful nature of reality while proclaiming himself fully liberated was more than Upaka could bear. Concluding that the fresh-faced Buddha's realization was only skin deep, he walked on by.

Upaka's rejection of the newly liberated Buddha was instructive. It helped the Buddha to frame his teachings in the manner that we now associate with him. There was no point describing his liberating vision off the bat; it was better to begin with suffering. From that point on, this was the Buddha's tactic. There is enough trauma in daily life to awaken the desire to be free, the Buddha taught. It is right here, already a part of us, already an underlying feeling in our lives. Painful experiences do not have to be cultivated specially—they do not have to be sought after or induced—there is already more than enough to go around. A willingness to face the feelings we already have is much more valuable than trying to escape from them (as the yoga practitioners of his time intended), exaggerate them (as the ascetics attempted), or minimize them altogether (as the materialists and laypeople tended to).

The Buddha applied this logic to both pleasure and pain. It is as silly to reject pleasurable feelings as it is to cultivate painful ones, he taught, but equally foolish to mindlessly pursue unstable pleasures in an attempt to blot out the anguish inherent to life. In later years, in the Buddhist cultures that grew up in India and then in Tibet, the word that was used to describe the world we inhabit translated as "tolerable," in the sense of being barely tolerable. The Buddha believed that this quality of "barely tolerable" was perfect for spiritual and psychological growth. The fragility of things is apparent to those who look, but if the mind can be taught to hold the instability with some measure of equanimity, a new kind of happiness reveals itself.

Because of his unvarying emphasis on *dukkha*, the Buddha's teachings were often taken to be pessimistic, as if he were still a practicing ascetic. But he was not. As Upaka recognized but could not embrace, Buddha rejected the cultivation of painful states. But he always claimed that, like a doctor, he had to be realistic. One can of course deceive with false consolation, denying the illness; or one may exaggerate the malady and give up hope completely.[4] But such a physician would be of little use. Buddha rejected these two extremes and continually applied the therapeutic middle. In a famous sutra, he compared himself to a surgeon pulling a poisonous arrow from a patient's flesh.[5] The tools he offered were powerful, but he admonished his listeners that even if the arrow were removed the patient could still die if he did not tend to the lesion himself. Even the best physician needs the cooperation of the patient, the Buddha affirmed. And every patient has to deal with his or her own wounds.

In today's world there are still contemporary versions of the ancient ascetics, with world views that are remarkably similar. Some of them remain in the wilds of India, living much as they did thousands of years ago, cultivating hardship in order to release themselves from the prisons of their attachments. But others are right here in our own culture. Today's examples include those who suffer from anorexia and starve themselves into an emaciated kind of invulnerability or those who hurt themselves, even cut themselves, to express and/or transcend inner wounds they are not entirely reconciled to. But there are many much less extreme but equally debilitating examples. People who are convinced of their own unworthiness, who cling, like my patient Monica, to the masts of their own insecurities, who are caught in one way or another by their negative feelings, bear close resemblance to the ascetics of the Buddha's time. Like his old friend Upaka, they have a very hard time seeing past their ingrained versions of reality, driven as they are by self-condemnation. As the comedian Louis C.K. has put it, in a contemporary twist on the Buddha's teachings, "Everything's amazing, and nobody's happy."

Therapists today, building on detailed observations of the infant-parent relationship, now have a way to explain this ascetic strain in the contemporary psyche. Their model, of "developmental trauma," is based on the realization that "there is no such thing as an infant"[6]; there is only a mother-child relationship. Infants are too dependent to be called persons in their own right—they survive only because their parents give themselves over to their care. This "relational" paradigm sees unbearable emotion as the determining factor in trauma. Intense feelings are present in a baby from birth. They take many forms—an infant's ruthless mix of appetite, need, and distress is well-known to any parent—and it is the parent's gut response to engage these rudimentary emotions and try to make them bearable, or barely tolerable, for their child. When this does not happen adequately, when the painful emotions or unpleasant feelings are not picked up and handled by the parents, the infant, or child, is left with overwhelming feelings he or she is not equipped to deal with, feelings that often get turned into self-hate.

My favorite example of this kind of parent-child attunement comes from a children's book one of my patients gave me after hearing me talk about this. The book is called *What's Wrong, Little Pookie?*[7] and in it a mother can be heard questioning her child about what is bothering him. She goes through a series of hypothetical questions (Are you hungry? Are you tired?) that become increasingly absurd (Did a very large hippo try to borrow your shoes?) until Little Pookie has completely forgotten why he was so upset in the first place. It is a humorous example of something parents do for their children all the time. They sense the emotional flavor of their child's mind and endeavor to help the child make sense of it, lightening the child's emotional load in the process.

"Painful or frightening affect becomes traumatic when the attunement that the child needs to assist in its tolerance, containment, and integration is profoundly absent,"[8] writes Robert Stolorow, a philosopher, psychologist, and clinical professor of psychiatry at UCLA, in his book about trauma. "One consequence of developmental trauma, relationally conceived, is that affect states take on enduring, crushing meanings. From recurring experiences of malattunement, the child acquires the unconscious conviction that unmet developmental yearnings and reactive painful feeling states are manifestations of a loathsome defect or of an inherent inner badness."

A recent patient of mine described a version of this perfectly. From as far back as she could remember, she had been convinced there was something wrong with her. This manifested in her preadolescent years as a conviction that her body was flawed. Her parents had their own problems, and she hid her feelings from them as best she could. But one consequence of this was that she not only felt that something was wrong with her but also blamed herself for feeling that way. She tried everything to get away from these uncomfortable feelings: ignoring them, rising above them, insulating herself from them, and pretending they were not there. None of these approaches worked too well—or, rather, they all worked a little. My patient grew to become an accomplished woman with a career and a family. But in private she was still troubled by self-negating feelings not entirely different from those she experienced as an adolescent. She could put up a good front now, but under the surface she was less than sanguine. Her body still bothered her. One day, when her college-aged children were home for the holidays, she was driving home feeling how quickly her life was passing her by. One moment her children were little and the next they were adults. Somehow, she let herself feel sad—an uncomfortable feeling she would not usually allow with such ease—and she sat in her driveway crying unabashedly before entering her home. When she told me about it some days later, she remarked upon how much worse the avoidance of the feelings was than the actual experience of them. She was touched in particular by how much love there was in her sadness.

One of the unintended consequences of this kind of story, and of the recent focus on developmental trauma in general, has been to encourage the fantasy that relief can come through identifying where, or with whom, one's trauma occurred. My patient and I both had the tendency to assign fault, if not to her then at least to her parents for having failed her. Although proponents of the relational perspective are quick to point out that "the possibility of emotional trauma is built into the basic constitution of human existence,"[9] it is still very tempting, when dealing with pain of this nature, to look for someone to blame. Disappointment is compounded when one discovers that tuning in to the lack of attunement does not, by itself, bring relief. The hope remains that by uncovering a single primal memory, or hearing a single insightful therapeutic interpretation, one will be healed.

One reason why I think the Buddha's loss of his mother makes sense as an organizing principle is that his loss occurred at such a young age. It would be impossible for him to remember it, and yet it is difficult to believe that it could have had no impact. While few of us suffer from this exact loss, many of us share the feelings of my patient, convinced that we are somehow flawed or defective. The psychotherapeutic model implies that it might have been possible for our families of origin to get it totally right: that if our parents had only been perfectly attuned to us we would feel okay. The quest for healing then takes off in a backward direction: toward the inevitable deprivations and deficiencies of the past. The Buddha did not imply that such deprivations did not matter—in fact his own experience suggests how central they can be—but he counseled a therapeutic approach that stayed relentlessly in the present. And he affirmed, in his First Noble Truth, that some residual feelings of deficiency are inevitable, no matter how good the parenting.

There is a beautiful example of what I take to be the Buddha's approach in a recent book about the poet Allen Ginsberg's first journey to India in 1961. Called *A Blue Hand*, Deborah Baker's work chronicles Ginsberg's early explorations of spiritual India, undertaken when he was in his early thirties. Ginsberg and several friends, including his longtime companion, Peter Orlovsky, spent their time in the company of whatever yogis, lamas, sadhus, charlatans, and saints they could find. In many ways, they were intent on uncovering what was left of the wild spiritual wilderness in which the Buddha wandered before his awakening. In one particularly poignant vignette toward the end of his odyssey, after a bitter fight with Orlovsky, Ginsberg had an encounter with a holy man named Devraha Baba in Benares, not far from where the Buddha gave his first teachings of the Four Noble Truths. A matted-haired, Shiva-worshipping ascetic whose only possessions were a deerskin rug, a wooden pot, a jute mat, and wooden sandals, Devraha Baba was famous for his irascibility. For example, when Indira Gandhi, the future prime minister of India, came to see him, sitting on a platform in the water on the far side of the Ganges River, he pointed the bottoms of his feet at her in the Indian gesture of contempt and refused to talk with her. But Ginsberg was given *darshan*, a chance to sit and talk with the Baba, although the exchange was interrupted when Devraha Baba, spotting Orlovsky in the distance, asked for him to come join their conversation. When Orlovsky refused, Devraha dismissed Ginsberg, telling him to come back when his friend was ready to join him. Ginsberg stayed put, however, and after some time of reflection in which he admitted to himself, perhaps for the first time, how he and Orlovsky had grown apart, he confessed his loneliness to Devraha Baba. Baker completes the story as follows:

> On his tiny platform suspended over the rushing waters of the Ganges, Devraha Baba looked at Allen. He tilted his head from side to side and sucked his teeth.
>
> "Oh!" he exclaimed. And with a tenderness that struck deep at Allen's heart, he said softly: "How wounded, how wounded."[10]

Devraha's intervention, subtle though it was, captures the essence of the Buddha's approach to developmental trauma. In his gentle, caring, but unsparing and unsentimental way, the Baba's retort helped bring Ginsberg's self-identification as a wounded soul into awareness. He focused all of his light on Ginsberg's darkest spot. The wounded nature of Ginsberg's self, originating perhaps in the childhood loss of his mother to psychosis but fed by the lability of his relationship with Orlovsky, may have been fundamental to Ginsberg's identity, but it was not something he had yet completely admitted to. Of note is the Baba's refusal to try to do anything about Ginsberg's plight. He did not counsel Ginsberg about his true nature, he did not urge him to meditate the feelings away, nor did he try to fill the emptiness of Ginsberg's soul. He simply noted the truth compassionately. To progress on the spiritual path, Ginsberg, who some years later embraced Buddhism, had to start where he was.

The observational posture that Buddhist psychology counsels is sometimes called bare attention. Its nakedness refers to the absence of reactivity in its response, to its pure and unadorned relatedness. Bare attention has been defined as the "clear and single-minded awareness of what happens to us and in us at the successive moments of perception."[11] In the Tibetan Buddhist tradition, this is sometimes evoked through the setting up of what is called a spy consciousness in the corner of the mind, watching or feeling everything that unfolds in the theater of the mind and body. Sometimes called mindfulness, it is described using metaphors ranging from climbing a tall water tower to look down from above to acting like a surgeon's probe, going deep into the afflicted area. This combination of detachment and engagement is characteristic of the attentional stance that is recommended. Bare attention also has a quality of renunciation to it. It asks us to defer our usual reactions in the service of something less egocentric; the instructions are not to cling to what is pleasant and not to reject what is unpleasant—to simply be with things as they are. If reactions occur (which they inevitably do), they too become grist for the mill, but they are never privileged. The idea is to let them settle down so that things can be known simply for what they are. This quality of renunciation is critical to the Buddha's method; it is what he learned from his six years of ascetic practices in the forest.

One of the central paradoxes of Buddhism is that the bare attention of the meditative mind changes the psyche by not trying to change anything at all. The steady application of the meditative posture, like the steadiness of an attuned parent, allows something inherent in the mind's potential to emerge, and it emerges naturally if left alone properly in a good enough way. When the Dalai Lama summarized his scholarly teachings on Buddhist thought with the paradoxical injunction "Transform your thoughts but remain as you are," he was pointing to this phenomenon. The thoughts he was after are rooted in the way we seek relief by finding someone or something to blame. The trauma within prompts us to search for a culprit, and we all too often attack ourselves or our loved ones in an attempt to eradicate the problem. This splitting of the self against itself or against its world only perpetuates suffering. The Buddha's method was to do something out of the ordinary, to make his mind like that of a mother: the most taken-for-granted person in our world but the missing ingredient in his. Adopting this stance creates room for a transformation that is waiting to happen, one that cannot occur unless one's inner environment is recalibrated in a specific way.

This understanding is not entirely outside the range of contemporary psychotherapy. It was articulated with great care by one of the first therapists to actually observe mothers interacting with their infants in a clinical setting. D. W. Winnicott, a British pediatrician and child analyst, wrote a lot about the quality of attunement he saw in "good-enough" mothers, a quality he called a mother's primary preoccupation:

> In this state mothers become able to put themselves into the infant's shoes, so to speak. That is to say, they develop an amazing capacity for identification with the baby, and this makes them able to meet the basic needs of the infant in a way that no machine can imitate, and no teaching can reach. . . .
>
> An infant who is held well enough is quite a different thing from one who has not been held well enough. . . . The reason why this special property of infant care must be mentioned, even in this brief statement, is that in the early stages of emotional development, before the senses have been organised, before there is something that could be called an autonomous ego, very severe anxieties are experienced. In fact, the word "anxiety" is of no use, the order of infant distress at this stage being of the same order as that which lies

behind panic, and panic is already a defence against the agony that makes people commit suicide rather than remember. I have meant to use strong language here. You see two infants; one has been held (in my extended sense of the word) well enough, and there is nothing to prevent a rapid emotional growth, according to inborn tendencies. The other has not had the experience of being held well and growth has had to be distorted and delayed, and some degree of primitive agony has to be carried on into life and living. Let it be said that in the common experience of good-enough holding the mother has been able to supply an auxiliary ego-function, so that the infant has had an ego from an early start, a very feeble, personal ego, but one boosted by the sensitive adaptation of the mother and by her ability to identify with her infant in relation to basic needs. The infant who has not had this experience has either needed to develop premature ego functioning, or else there has developed a muddle.[12]

Primitive agony was one of Winnicott's most important concepts; it was the aspect of the Buddha's *dukkha* that he was most attuned to. In describing how a mother helps her child get to know feelings through her holding of him, Winnicott also painted the picture of how it must feel for an infant to be deprived of such holding. He spoke of an order of distress behind panic and deliberately conjured suicide as an expression of the inexpressible agony an infant faces if left too much in the dark. While he stressed that most parents protect their children as best they can from such feelings, he also implied that such anxieties were always lurking. Like the relational therapists who followed in his wake, he was attuned to the "enduring, crushing meanings" unbearable affect states could evoke. His insights help explain a hidden and powerful aspect of the therapy the Buddha devised. Whether or not the historical Buddha actually suffered from the kind of primitive agonies Winnicott expounded upon, the meditations he taught in the aftermath of his awakening "hold" the mind just as Winnicott described a mother "holding" an infant. In making the observational posture of mindfulness central to his technique, the Buddha established another version of "an auxiliary ego-function" in the psyches of his followers, one that enabled them, to go back to his metaphor of pulling out an arrow, to tend to their own wounds with both their minds and their hearts. Far from eliminating the ego, as I naively believed I should when I first began to practice meditation, the Buddha encouraged a strengthening of the ego so that it could learn to hold primitive agonies without collapse.

A friend of mine who spent years in India with a great teacher from the ancient forest tradition tells a moving story that, to my mind, makes the same point. Years after his beloved teacher had died, he was back in India staying at the home of his guru's most devoted Indian disciple.

"I must show you something," the disciple said to my friend one day. "This is what he left for me." My friend was excited, of course. Any trace of his teacher was nectar to him. He watched as the elderly man opened the creaking doors of an ancient wooden wardrobe and took something from the back of the bottom shelf. It was wrapped in an old, dirty cloth.

"Do you see?" he asked my friend.

"No. See what?"

The disciple unwrapped the object, revealing an old, beat-up aluminum pot, the kind of ordinary pot one sees in every Indian kitchen. Looking deeply into my friend's eyes, he told him, "He left this for me when he went away. Do you see? Do you see?"

"No, Dada," he replied. "I don't see."

According to my friend, Dada looked at him even more intensely, this time with a mad glint in his eyes.

"You don't have to shine," he said. "*You don't have to shine*."[13] He rewrapped the pot and put it back on the bottom shelf of the wardrobe.

My friend had received the most important teaching, one that had its origins in the Buddha's revolutionary approach. He did not have to transform himself in the way he imagined: He just had to learn to be kind to himself. If he could hold himself with the care Dada showed while clutching the old pot, it would be enough. His ordinary self, wrapped in all of its primitive agony, was precious too.

3

Everything Is Burning

The Buddha did shine, of course, as his erstwhile friend Upaka could not help but notice. One of the names he was called in the ancient sutras was "Aṅgirasa": he who shines brilliantly, while emitting multicolored flames, or rays of light, from his body.[1] It might be hard to reconcile the Buddha's shining countenance with what my friend learned in India about leaving his unpolished flaws alone, but the two are actually related. The Buddha shone because the fires of his own attachments blew out. He was not trying to shine: It happened when he stopped fighting with himself, when he became able to hold his anguish as tenderly as Dada held that old aluminum pot his guru had left for him.

The Buddha began to talk about this almost immediately after his enlightenment. Newly awakened and finding the voice that came to be called his "Lion's Roar," he began to put words on his breakthrough. He followed up his first sermon, the one on the Four Noble Truths given to his five former friends on the outskirts of Benares, with his next-most-famous teaching, known colloquially as the Fire Sermon. While the first teaching had been given almost privately to his five former companions, this one had an audience of a thousand matted-haired, fire-worshipping ascetics, drawn like moths to a flame.

News of the Buddha's attainments had spread fast. Camps of wandering sadhus coalesced around him, curious to see what he was made of. The Buddha, as was his wont, engaged them by focusing on what they were most attached to and most interested in. In a rare exercise of his miraculous powers, he made it impossible for them to tend their sacred fires without his intervention. When they tried to split their logs according to the apocryphal story, they could not, until the Buddha said the magic word. When they tried to light their fires, they were similarly restrained, and when they tried to put their fires out, they could not do that either. The Buddha even materialized five hundred braziers for the ascetics to warm themselves with in the midst of the coldest winter night and then pushed back the floodwaters after a terrible storm so that he could walk on dry ground. The ancient sutras spell out these displays as if they were facts, but the miraculous feats were not the main point. The Buddha was speaking the fire worshippers' language. He knew how to get their attention. Having roused their curiosity, he offered them a teaching. He then took their devotion to their sacred fires and turned it inside out. He had done the same thing in his first talk by giving new meaning to the word "noble," which until that point had been used exclusively to demarcate the upper-caste Brahmins in ancient India's stratified society. The noble person wasn't noble by virtue of the caste he was born into, the Buddha suggested then; he was noble because he could see the truth. Nobility came from within, he insisted; it was not a product of one's hereditary place in society.

In the case of the Fire Sermon, the Buddha did something similar. Whether or not he actually performed physical miracles, he did something miraculous with his language. He took the literal meaning of the word "fire" and turned it into a metaphor. The actual translation of the sutra's Pali name, *Āditta-pariyāya*, is "The Way of Putting Things as Being on Fire," which conveys the Buddha's metaphorical intent.[2] The matted-haired ascetics, ritualistically tending their sacred fires, were missing the point. Rather than being so concrete about it, he suggested to the mass of *bhikkhus*, or mendicants (literally, ones who live by alms), arrayed before him, that they should see the flames all around them. Everyday life is a trauma, the Buddha proclaimed: It is as if everything is burning. He spoke of trauma as if it were a fire.

> Bhikkhus, all is burning. And what is all that is burning?
>
> The eye is burning. Visible forms are burning. Eye-consciousness is burning. Eye-contact is burning. Also feeling, whether pleasant or painful or neither-painful-nor-pleasant, that too is burning. Burning with what? Burning with the fire of lust, with the fire of hate, with the fire of delusion; it is burning with birth, ageing and death, with sorrow, lamentation, pain, grief and despair, I say.
>
> The ear is burning. Sounds are burning. . . .
>
> The nose is burning. Odors are burning. . . .
>
> The tongue is burning. Flavors are burning. . . .
>
> The body is burning. Tangibles are burning. . . .
>
> The mind is burning. Mental objects are burning.[3]

With this single metaphor, the Buddha managed to consolidate the most important strands of his thought. He took the sacred fires of his listeners and not only put them out but stripped them of their idealized status. Rites and rituals will get you nowhere, he declared. And he used his metaphorical imagery to drive home his vision of the ubiquity of trauma. Everyday life is on fire not only because of how fleeting it is, which we know but don't like to admit, but also because of how ardently we cling to our own greed, anger, and egocentric preoccupations. He called these the "three fires," in another punning play on the three "sacrificial fires" a devout Brahmin householder was committed to tending daily.[4] We don't have to tend the fires purposively and obsessively, he told his listeners—we are constantly feeding the three egocentric fires unconsciously. Hundreds of years later, when the semantic origins of the "three fires" were long forgotten, greed, hatred, and delusion came to be known in the Buddhist world as the three "poisons," but this was not a word that the Buddha actually used. His initial language, while strong, was more forgiving than that. Subliminally, the Buddha was saying, we are all tending these fires (of greed, hatred, and delusion), motivated as we are by our insecure place in the world, by the feeling, the *dukkha*, of not fitting in. The fires of greed, hatred, and delusion are defenses against acknowledging that everything is on fire, instinctive attempts at protecting ourselves from what feels like an impossible situation. The Buddha stressed the burning nature of the world in order to show his listeners what they were afraid of. By placing their spiritual aspirations outside themselves they were shoring up their egocentric defenses. Only by looking into the traumas they were made of could they find release.

He continued to use this imagery when describing his awakening. "Nirvāna" (*nibbāna* in Pali) means "going out." The word is derived from the Sanskrit root *vā*, meaning "to blow," and the prefix *nir*, meaning "cease to burn" or "go out" (like a flame).[5] But the verb is intransitive and—this is important—it means that there is no agent doing the blowing, no *one* who causes the flame to go out. "Nirvāna" means "going out": It just happens when conditions are right; no one makes it happen. The fires of trauma—of greed, hatred, and delusion and of birth, aging, and death—are self-liberating. They blow out when conditions in the mind are right. The first step, as the Buddha described in the Fire Sermon, is to deal with the fear we harbor about the traumatic nature of things. This fear leads us either to ignore the flames we are made of or to hope that, through some magic, it might be possible to get rid of them altogether. But the flames can go out only when we stop pretending they are not there.

As moving as this aspect of the Fire Sermon may be, this is not the end of the Buddha's use of the metaphor. It is the so-called negative view of nirvana but not the only way of describing it. The positive view points to the underlying nature of reality. It tends to imply, erroneously, that nirvana is a place or a state to be achieved, something apart from the everyday world. Nevertheless, at times the Buddha leaned toward this description. He used a different word, one that sounded similar but came from different roots and carried a vastly different meaning (*nirvṛti* in Sanskrit *or nibbuti* in Pali). *Nirvṛti* means "bliss,"[6] and there is a related word meaning "blissful" that describes how the world appears when the wisdom eye is opened. "When the fires of passion, hatred and delusion die out within one," writes Richard Gombrich, one of Oxford's foremost scholars of the Buddha's thought, "one experiences bliss."[7] Everything is burning, then, not only with impermanence and pain but also with bliss. The vision of one leads to the knowledge of the other.

In spelling out the connection between acknowledging trauma and experiencing its release, the Buddha was describing something that today's psychotherapists have also found. I had a serendipitous discussion with a friend of mine recently that encapsulates the connection. My wife and I were having brunch with another couple and talking about what we were all working on. I was trying to describe this particular Buddhist concept, the one I am writing about here: that the blissful nature of reality is part and parcel of the fact that everything is burning. I used the shorthand phrase, common in Buddhist circles but unfamiliar to my friends, "nirvana is samsara, samsara is nirvana" to describe it. "Saṃsāra" is the Sanskrit word for the cycle of rebirth. It means "keeping going"[8] and connotes the everyday world of conventional suffering driven by egocentric preoccupation. The idea is that nirvana is not a separate place that we can get to when we eliminate what we don't like about ourselves but is already here, hidden behind our likes and dislikes, in the everyday.

My friend, unfamiliar with my Buddhist lingo, thought I said, "Nirvana is some sorrow, some sorrow is nirvana." She had a flash of insight and thought she understood what I meant. She had recently started group therapy and discovered that, in her tendency to try to make everything okay for everyone, she was avoiding her own anger. Acknowledging her anger in therapy had opened up a feeling of sadness, a willingness to own the feelings of disappointment or betrayal she sometimes felt, and felt ashamed of. Like my patient who had cried and cried in her car when feeling the fleeting nature of her life but had been moved by the love her sorrow contained, my friend at brunch understood that acknowledging her sorrow opened her in a deeper way than was possible by always trying to be "nice." There was a freedom in "some sorrow" that gave her a brief hint of nirvana.

Trauma experts report something similar. "It cannot be overemphasized that injurious childhood experiences in and of themselves need not be traumatic (or at least not lastingly so) or pathogenic provided that they occur within a responsive milieu. *Pain is not pathology.* It is the absence of adequate attunement and responsiveness to the child's painful emotional reactions that renders them unendurable and thus a source of traumatic states and psychopathology."[9] The Buddha was after something similar in his Fire Sermon. The burning, fleeting nature of reality is not pathological, he was saying: It just is. If you create an atmosphere of attunement and responsiveness within yourself, one that mimics the mental and emotional state of an attentive parent, this pain and sorrow becomes not only endurable but self-liberating. It releases, and in the process, we can also be released.

This phenomenon plays out in the realm of the everyday as well.

No matter how hard we try to make a world that is rational, predictable, and under our control, things still go wrong. Traumas, big and small, are constantly interfering with our lives. If they are not befalling us, they are happening to our neighbors, and we have a choice in how we react. We can pretend they are not happening or we can meet them with attunement and responsiveness. A friend of mine was flying to Europe recently from New York. He got to Kennedy airport two hours ahead of his flight's scheduled departure and waited for a good forty-five minutes in a huge line to check in. The clerk took one look at his ticket and told him, unceremoniously, that his flight was leaving from Newark, not from JFK. He had just enough time to race there by taxi to make his flight. Otherwise he would have to buy a new ticket.

Berating himself and fueled with adrenaline, he ran to the front of the long taxi queue and pleaded his case with the woman at the head of the line. "Could I please step in front of you?" he asked her, his voice cracking. "I went to the wrong airport and I might be able to make it to Newark in time for my flight if I leave right now." His trauma was in vivid display but the woman responded coldly. "Do you know how long I've been waiting here?" she scolded. "You may not cut in front of me. You should wait your turn." The taxi dispatcher overheard my friend's plea, however, and called out to him. Pointing to a cab that someone was just getting into, he waved my friend over. "Hurry up," he said. "That person is going to Newark Airport, too. Get in." My friend made it there just in time, his trauma ameliorated by the kindness of a stranger.

This kind of trauma is happening all of the time, all around us. When the Buddha taught the Fire Sermon he was pointing this out. When we resist the underlying traumatic nature of things, we cut ourselves off from ourselves and from others. We become like the woman at the head of the line, jealously guarding our positions and impervious to the struggles of others. But when we accept the presence of some sorrow, we can embody the bliss of the taxi dispatcher, spontaneously responding to those truly in need.

One of the most famous stories in the Buddhist literature also speaks to the ubiquity of trauma and weaves in the lesson of the Fire Sermon while playing on the notion of the Buddha as a physician. The tale is of a mother, Kisagotami, whose infant son had suddenly died of illness. Kisagotami's predicament was all too vivid. Her son had died but she refused to put down his body. Bereft and on the edge of madness, she wandered through her village clutching the dead child to her breast, a stunning manifestation of grief and trauma. She begged every person she met to find her a doctor, someone to bring her baby back to life. The villagers were frightened of her and turned away. She became more and more desperate, more and more agitated, more and more distressed. Finally, one man took pity on her and told her that he had heard of someone with medicine for this kind of thing. She went to the Buddha, told her story, and listened to his response.

"Yes," he said, "I have medicine for this. But first bring me some mustard seed from a house where no one has died."

Kisagotami went back to the village and knocked on door after door. "The living are few but the dead are many," she was told. She could not find a house that had not known death, and she returned to the Buddha without any mustard seed to seek further advice, having put her baby down in the forest before returning. It is notable both what the Buddha said and what he did not say. He did not tell Kisagotami that this was her karma and that she must accept it. He did not tell her that she must have done something terrible in a past life to deserve such a fate. In a famous sutra, preserved in the collection called *Saṃyutta Nikāya*, he explicitly rejected such a naive view of karma. In that sutra, when asked directly whether all of the painful things that happen to a person are a result of karma, he answered in the negative. "That would be overshooting," he said. "Only one in eight such things are due to karma."

"You know the feeling of too much bile?" he asked his interlocutor. That feeling is due to a physical imbalance, not to a negative intention or an unwholesome thought or an unethical action. There are other such imbalances that cause disease and these, too, are outside our control. Similarly, he went on, there are unfortunate things that can occur because of the weather. Floods, earthquakes, droughts, and so on happen according to their own laws—it is not right to suggest that victims of them are in any way responsible or that they somehow created their fate. Other adversities are similarly random. Even acts of violence are not the result of karma, he continued. We often fall prey to them inadvertently, not because of anything we have said or done but simply because we are in the wrong place at the wrong time.[10]

The Buddha said a simple thing to Kisagotami when she returned to him. "You thought that you alone had lost a son. The law of death is that among all living creatures there is no permanence."[11] He was not lecturing Kisagotami at this point. She was already transformed. Her engagement with the people of the village had developed her empathy. Instead of relating to them solely from a place of her own suffering, she had been inquiring after their own experiences of life and death. In seeing that she was not the only one to undergo such pain, she became more able to see the impermanent nature of everything. The Buddha was acknowledging the reality she had already glimpsed. He did not try to tell her the "truth" before she was ready.

Later, after having taken the robes of a *bhikkuni*, or female mendicant, Kisagotami was outside on a hillside at nightfall gazing at the village below. She saw the lights in the village dwellings flickering on and off and had a sudden realization, one that consolidated everything that had come before. "My state is like those lamps," she thought, and the Buddha shot her a vision of himself at that moment to affirm her insight.

"All living beings resemble the flame of these lamps," he told her, "one moment lighted, the next extinguished—those only who have arrived at Nirvana are at rest."[12] Just as he did in the Fire Sermon, the Buddha articulated his central message. The parallel between the Buddha's approach and that of today's trauma therapists is clear. Even in this most undeniably painful circumstance, when dealing with the loss of a child, *pain is not pathology*. By creating an inner environment of attunement and responsiveness, even this most unendurable and crushing reality became not only bearable but illuminating.

I was reminded of these connections recently by another patient, Alexa, an inspiring thirty-five-year-old writer who told me how upset she had been with herself for uncharacteristically losing her temper with her three-year-old son one busy weekday morning. Her story was not atypical for parents of toddlers: Her beloved child was beginning to wear her out. She was trying to get him dressed and fed and out of the house, and he was frustrating her at every turn, not wanting to put on his shoes, taking off pieces of clothing when she turned her back, asking her to play a favorite game with him, and altogether refusing to cooperate with her pleas. Having made it through his terrible twos, she was not yet prepared for how trying his threes could be. Exasperated, Alexa had unloaded on him.

"You think the world revolves around you, and it doesn't," she cried impatiently.

There was a brief pause in which he gazed at her wide-eyed.

"It moves, Momma?" he replied.

His earnest cry cut short her irritation, of course, and rekindled her delight in him. She still remembers the guilt she felt, though. Why would she want to say such a thing? How could she shatter his safe world view in an instant out of anger? His words functioned a little bit like a Zen master's response, his innocent question stopping her in her tracks. "How does he even know that revolve means move?" she remembers asking herself.

Alexa had successfully created a world for her son of which he *was* the center—her exasperated comment only affirmed how productive she had been at fostering this illusion. Her son had what therapists call a healthy attachment to his mother; he was able to take her support entirely for granted; she had given him the attunement and responsiveness necessary to ward off most developmental trauma. She had wanted him to feel like he was the center of the world, and she had succeeded, and she was right to have done so. As today's therapists conceive of it, her first major task as a mother was mostly done. The second task, of gradually easing her child into "disillusionment," of failing him just enough that he could begin to know her as a separate person and relate to her empathically, could only be undertaken if and when the first mission was accomplished successfully.

Winnicott described this double mission of the mother with his usual poetic intensity:

> The mother, at the beginning, by an almost 100 per cent adaptation affords the infant the opportunity for the *illusion* that her breast is part of the infant. It is, as it were, under the baby's magical control. The same can be said in terms of infant care in general, in the quiet times between excitements. Omnipotence is nearly a fact of experience. The mother's eventual task is gradually to disillusion the infant, but she has no hope of success unless at first she has been able to give sufficient opportunity for illusion.[13]

It was my guess that the unexpected friction between Alexa and her son heralded the beginning of a disillusioning process that would likely proceed as smoothly as the first several years had gone. Her son's unexpected reply, however, tapped into another kind of truth, one closer to the Buddha's Fire Sermon. The world, despite our mothers' best attempts to shield us, *does* move: incessantly, unpredictably, and without regard for our feelings. As human beings, raised, if we are lucky, to be the centers of our own little worlds, we are continually taken aback by this reality, even if we have been successfully cared for by our good-enough parents. The Buddha, whose meditations resurrect the holding environment and auxiliary ego-function of the good-enough mother, also served as parent in this important way. As he made clear in the Fire Sermon, he did not shrink from disillusioning people who still harbored the impression that the world revolved around them.

It is in this way that the Buddha's teachings speak directly to the trauma of everyday life. The quality of bare attention, the nonjudgmental and nonreactive observation that parallels the noninterfering attention of the good-enough mother, is just the first step of the Buddha's approach. As everyone knows, the role of the mother changes as the child grows. While the basic stance persists, it also matures along with the child. At the right time, the good-enough mother cannot help but begin to disillusion her child. Like Alexa, she just can't take it anymore. She becomes able to use her anger at her child, and her child's aggression, to help her child grow. In a similar manner, the observational neutrality of the meditative mind is not neutral when it comes to the ego. Selfishness, conceit, pride, jealousy, and envy are observed without surprise, but they are not indulged. Instead, much as a mother might gently tease a child who is excessively demanding of his or her own way, the meditative mind delights in frustrating the clamoring ego's insistent demands. This, too, is a therapeutic function, one the Buddha carefully cultivated in all of his teachings.

I once had the chance to speak with a renowned Thai forest master named Ajahn Chah directly about all this. It was more than thirty years ago, but I remember his words as if it were yesterday. I was traveling in Asia with some of my first American Buddhist teachers and we had made our way to Ajahn Chah's monastery on the Lao border of Thailand. Ajahn Chah met with us after we shared the monastery lunch. We asked him to explain the Buddhist view. What had he learned from his years of contemplation and study? What could we bring back to share with the West? His answer touched my own sense of residual trauma, my own fear of everything burning.

Before saying a word, he motioned to a glass at his side. "Do you see this glass?" he asked us. "I love this glass. It holds the water admirably. When the sun shines on it, it reflects the light beautifully. When I tap it, it has a lovely ring. Yet for me, this glass is already broken. When the wind knocks it over or my elbow knocks it off the shelf and it falls to the ground and shatters, I say, 'Of course.' But when I understand that this glass is already broken, every minute with it is precious."

This spontaneous bit of wisdom struck me deeply and has stayed with me over the years. I often refer to it when teaching. Ajahn Chah was capturing the Buddhist insight into the impermanence of things but not falling into the abyss of negating them utterly. He was giving another version of the Fire Sermon where everything is broken but everything is also dear. What was he referring to exactly? The glass, the body, this life, the self? The implication seemed clear enough: The self, like the glass, doesn't exist in the way we imagine it—it doesn't exist in the way we wish it did. But by acknowledging this reality up front, Ajahn Chah was modeling a different way of relating.

We could use, appreciate, value, and respect the glass without expecting it to last. In fact, we could use it more freely, with more abandon and more care, once we understood that it lacked what Buddhists call inherent existence. The glass, like the self, does not lose its value when we understand that it is on fire.

Speaking in the vernacular of his own time and place, and going completely against the norm, the Buddha systematically took apart all conventional notions of permanence. He insisted that there was no eternal essence in a human being, for example, no spirit that was one with God, no immortal soul that survives death, and no sacred fire that must be tended. Even consciousness cannot be shown to exist independently, he claimed. Nothing exists in its own right or under its own power. We emerge, as infants, from a relational matrix and then struggle to come to terms with the trauma of aloneness. While all things remain contingent, relative, and relational, our object-seeking instincts desire a security we assume is our birthright. As a patient of mine, Carl, once ruefully said, in describing how tenaciously he could cling to unavailable women who were turned off by his neediness, "I'm scared to lose what I don't have." The Buddha said much the same thing about the rest of us. We cling to a notion of permanence that, according to Buddha, never existed in the first place. We cling to a glass that is already broken.

Many people suffer because of failures in their infancies, failure to be made sufficiently secure in the illusion of their centrality, failure to have a taste of boundless support[14] from their parental environments. Such people, when they dig down to their core, find feelings of absence, feelings of lack, feelings of impotence or rage where once there might have been omnipotence. Others suffer because of failures in the disillusioning process itself—as adults they clamor for attention from their loved ones, expecting these people to be as selfless as their mothers once were, and they become punitive when they do not get their way. They insist on always being the center of attention and find it difficult to connect empathically with others. Their perpetual feeling of disillusion is evidence of their failure to be disillusioned. Still others manage to weather the travails of early childhood, of illusion and disillusion. But many of these people, despite the relative ease of

46

their childhoods, nevertheless come to feel like my patient Monica, nostalgic for the glow of her mother's love while uncomfortably alone and adrift in what seems a hostile universe.

The incessant movement of the world does not have to intimidate us, the Buddha proclaimed in his Fire Sermon. We are all part of it, even if our notions of self-help suggest that we should be able to rise above it. Shinnying up the masts of our selves in order to escape from the pain all around us, we succeed only in reinforcing our not-so-secret feelings of dread. Alone at the top of the mast, we remain entangled in our tangles, burning with the three fires of greed, hatred, and delusion. The Buddha had something else in mind for us, something that Western therapists have also begun to figure out. Look closely at this world, he suggested. Examine it carefully. Probe your experience deeply, with attunement and responsiveness, and you may come to agree with me. Like the glass, this world is already broken. And yet when you drop your fear and open your heart, its preciousness is there too.

The implications for daily life are manifold. With broken selves in a world on fire, trauma is everywhere. Bob Dylan, on his weekly satellite radio show, once quoted Richard Gere quoting the Dalai Lama quoting the eighth-century Indian Buddhist Shantideva, author of the classic *Guide to the Bodhisattva's Way of Life*, on this point.

"If you want to be happy," Dylan hissed, "practice compassion. If you want others to be happy, practice compassion." Only Dylan could manage to make the word compassion sound sinister, although I think he was channeling something of the Buddha's Fire Sermon when he did. If everything is burning, the compassionate gaze of a parent is a natural response to the flames that engulf us. There is sorrow in samsara, indeed, but also bliss.

The Rush to Normal

The Buddha did not always know that the world was on fire. Nor did he always have a feel for its bliss. He lived his first twenty-nine years in a kind of protective bubble, not looking too much beneath the surface of things. There was a deliberate agenda on the part of his family to keep him sheltered from the outside world, much as overprotective parents of our own time try to insulate their children from the pressures they fear will overtake them, but he was also compliant with their agenda, up to a point. He had a luxurious life, with all of his needs taken care of and only the vaguest hint of unease. It is generally accepted that, apart from his infantile experience of loss, the young Buddha-to-be made it to his twenty-ninth year without ever seeing death, sickness, or decrepitude. As the story is told, only when journeying outside the palace walls in an unusual expedition with his faithful groom did the Buddha catch glimpses of a corpse, a sickly person, a stooped and aged one, and a forest recluse. So startled was he said to be by these "Four Messengers" that he resolved to leave his privileged life to seek one of wandering austerity.

As safe and protected as he may have been throughout the first third of his life, the earliest days of his infancy were tumultuous. There was trouble from the start. Strange omens accompanied his birth, and the strangeness continued into his first week of life. His mother, Maya, said by legend to be a local queen, dreamed of being nuzzled by a white elephant on the night of his conception and delivered her baby from her side exactly ten months after her nocturnal vision. Standing in a fragrant grove of fruit-laden trees called Lumbini, a half day's journey from the town of Kapilavatthu, where she lived, she steadied herself by grasping a low-hanging limb of a *sala* tree with her uplifted right arm and gazed at the sky as her child was drawn through her right side from her womb. According to legend, he was placed, standing on two feet, on the ground, where he precociously took seven steps to the north, lifted one arm, pointed his finger to the sky, and proclaimed something on the order of "I'm the one!"

One early collection of Buddhist stories, the *Jātaka*, describes how the Buddha and his mother were honored in the immediate aftermath of his birth by two showers of water, one warm and one cool, descending from the sky onto their bodies. And shortly after this heavenly bath, a wise man named Asita, one of those mountain *rishis*, or recluses, who populate the Indian landscape, had a vision while in retreat that a great being had been born. He found his way to the family and, recognizing a series of signs and marks upon the infant's body, prophesied to his parents that the child would become either a great monarch or a renowned spiritual leader. The joy he felt at discovering such a child was soon tempered by grief as he recognized that he, already old, would be dead before this great being would begin to teach or lead. As Asita began to weep uncontrollably at his realization, the young Buddha's father became frightened.

"What's wrong?" the father implored him. "Will something terrible come to pass?"

"No, no," Asita reassured him, "there will be no misfortune. But a person of this caliber is unlikely to settle for the role of great monarch." Tears streaming down his face, Asita took leave of the family, the birth of the infant already tarnished by thoughts of impending death.

Three days later, the Buddha's mother, Maya, died. The newborn, after exclaiming that he was the one, now suddenly was. The only one. Half of a mother–infant dyad, surrounded by surrogates but cut off from the most important person in his young life.

How would he have coped? The rest of his family did not abandon him. They gathered round, gave him wet nurses to suckle on, an aunt to care for him, cousins to play with, and servants to attend to his needs. His father immediately entrusted the baby's care to his wife's sister, to whom he was already married, and she raised the infant lovingly as her own. But his father was unnerved by all that had happened in the space of the single week. The sudden and inexplicable loss of his beloved wife, on the heels of Asita's uncanny weeping, had cast a pall over the entire birth. "A shadow of awe and uncertainty"[1] settled over the Buddha's father, and he resolved then and there to keep his son from abandoning him as his wife already had. He would give him every luxury, indulge his every whim. "If the prince found nothing more to wish for, the king thought, the notion of abandoning the palace would never occur to him."[2]

The Buddha, some years after forsaking his wife, newborn son, father, palace, and extended family despite his father's best-laid plans, thought back to what his childhood had been like. His recollection functions as a kind of screen memory, telegraphing meaning beyond its immediate associations. In his reflection, the Buddha described how fragile he had felt as a child, how protected he had been from the basic sufferings of old age, illness, and death, and how at some point the protective edifice around him began to crumble. It is a good description of what today's child therapists might call the first cracks in his grandiosity or his childhood omnipotence, cracks that usually come around the age of two or three but that, in the story that grew up around the Buddha, seem to have been delayed. In his reflection, we can see him getting a glimmer of disillusionment, realizing in a preliminary way that the world, despite his father's best intentions, did not revolve around him. The passage links his dawning self-awareness with a nascent capacity for empathy and reveals, from a Buddhist perspective, how each emboldens the other. It was one of the few times in which the Buddha spoke of his own state of mind while growing up, and it hints at the pressures gnawing at him in the midst of his otherwise privileged upbringing.

Here is how he described himself preserved in the Pali Canon, said by its adherents to contain the complete teachings of the Buddha, preserved in the language they were first written down in, several hundred years after a great council that followed his death. In this passage, recorded in the *Anguttara Nikāya*, the Buddha reflects on the life his father and aunt created for him and gives a hint of his burgeoning discontent.

I was delicate, most delicate, supremely delicate. Lily pools were made for me at my father's house solely for my benefit. Blue lilies flowered in one, white lilies in another, red lilies in a third. I used no sandalwood that was not from Benares. My turban, tunic, lower garments and cloak were all made of Benares cloth. A white sunshade was held over me day and night so that no cold or heat or dust or grit or dew might inconvenience me.

I had three palaces; one for the winter, one for the summer and one for the rains. In the rains palace I was entertained by minstrels with no men among them. For the four months of the rains I never went down to the lower palace. Though meals of broken rice with lentil soup are given to the servants and retainers in other people's houses, in my father's house white rice and meat was given to them.[3]

It is startling to hear the Buddha speaking of his delicate nature. The images that we have of him—as prince, warrior, forest recluse, and awakened sage—do not correspond. Yet as he makes clear further along in his reflections, he is clearly pointing to something central to his preenlightenment personality. Not only was he spoiled, he was also vain and insecure. Protected from any knowledge of mortality, he was perched on a precarious foundation. Having been led to think of himself as virtually immortal, at his core he felt himself to be as delicate as his surroundings.

In the rest of this critical and revealing passage, right on the heels of describing his delicate nature, the Buddha remembered the moment when he first caught sight of his ego, struggling to maintain its hegemony. He described his first inklings of insight and the first cracks in what a psychoanalyst would call his "false self." He also made clear the connection between these insights and the dawning of his ability to relate sympathetically to others.

Whilst I had such power and good fortune, yet I thought: "When an untaught ordinary man, who is subject to ageing, not safe from ageing, sees another who is aged, he is shocked, humiliated and disgusted; for he forgets that he himself is no exception. But I too am subject to ageing, not safe from ageing, and so it cannot befit me to be shocked, humiliated and disgusted on seeing another who is aged." When I considered this, the vanity of youth entirely left me.

I thought: "When an untaught ordinary man, who is subject to sickness, not safe from sickness, sees another who is sick, he is shocked, humiliated and disgusted; for he forgets that he himself is no exception. But I too am subject to sickness, not safe from sickness, and so it cannot befit me to be shocked, humiliated and disgusted on seeing another who is sick." When I considered this, the vanity of health entirely left me.

I thought: "When an untaught ordinary man, who is subject to death, not safe from death, sees another who is dead, he is shocked, humiliated and disgusted, for he forgets that he himself is no exception. But I too am subject to death, not safe from death, and so it cannot befit me to be shocked, humiliated and disgusted on seeing another who is dead." When I considered this, the vanity of life entirely left me.[4]

In later iterations, these reflections on the vanities of youth, health, and life were combined with other traditional stories to yield the more familiar tale of the future Buddha's disillusionment with his overly protected world. In these later versions of his story, Gotama (the Buddha's given name) was taken out beyond the palace walls by his charioteer Channa and on each occasion was confronted with aspects of life his protective father had prevented him from knowing. But it is interesting that this familiar story appears in the Pali Canon only in a legendary recounting of a *past* Buddha's life story, never as part of the current Buddha's history. Many scholars believe that the former Buddha's story was recruited at a later time to explain the Buddha's motivation for leaving home. But the above passage is the closest the traditional Canon comes to explaining his disillusionment with his protective upbringing, and it sheds a great deal of light on the Buddha's inner predicament. There are obvious parallels between this passage and the traditional story of the Four Messengers, but the version in the Pali Canon points to the inner reflection the Buddha engaged in. He was clearly wrestling with himself and with the defensive shroud that had been thrown around him. He had been raised to think that trauma did not exist, that nothing out of the ordinary could ever happen to him, that he would always be maintained in his state of grace. But just beneath the surface was a trauma that had already taken place, one that his father was trying to forget and hoped the young child would never have to deal with. On one level, this is an unbelievable story, so gilded as to make it impossible to relate to. Who could reach the age of twenty-nine and never consider the possibility of old age, disease, or death? But on another level, the kind of denial that cloaked the Buddha is akin to that which we all use to live our lives without collapsing.

Therapists who specialize in the treatment of trauma spell this out clearly. They speak of how trauma robs its victims of the "absolutisms" of daily life: the myths we live by that allow us to go to sleep at night trusting we will still be there in the morning. In their use of the word "absolutism" these therapists reveal an important link between ancient Buddhist philosophy and today's psychotherapies. The Buddha, after his awakening, emphasized over and over again the contingent nature of the universe: the transient, chaotic, and impersonal flux he summarized in the sutra entitled "The Way of Putting Things as Being on Fire." But before his awakening, as revealed in the passages about his delicate nature, he was a living example of the perils and promises of one who subscribes to the absolutisms of daily life. We all need these absolutisms to survive, and yet they are inevitably challenged by the realities of life over which we have little control. Trauma lurks behind every corner. Even if we are closed up behind the walls of a palace, our own self-reflective thoughts eventually puncture the reassuring facade that surrounds us.

"When a person says to a friend, 'I'll see you later,' or a parent says to a child at bedtime, 'I'll see you in the morning,' these are statements, like delusions, whose validity is not open to discussion. Such absolutisms are the basis for a kind of naïve realism and optimism that allows one to function in the world, experienced as stable and predictable. It is in the essence of emotional trauma that it shatters these absolutisms, a catastrophic loss of innocence that permanently alters one's sense of being-in-the-world."[5] Traumatized people are left with an experience of "singularity" that creates a divide between their experience and the consensual reality of others. Part of what makes it traumatic is the lack of communication that is possible about it. "The worlds of traumatized persons are fundamentally incommensurable with those of others," Robert Stolorow writes. Trauma creates a "deep chasm in which an anguished sense of estrangement and solitude takes form."[6] I have seen this over and over again in patients of mine who have undergone direct trauma, those who have been in war zones, lost family members to accidents or disease, or become terminally ill. They are suddenly dropped into an alternate reality that feels as "singular" as Kisagotami's did when she lost her infant son. After 9/11, for example, a middle-aged patient with a terminal illness, whom I had been seeing for about a year while he underwent various experimental treatments, felt suddenly vindicated. "Now everyone's feeling what I've been feeling," he said, smiling numbly. He lived in my neighborhood, several blocks from the World Trade Center, and he was absolutely fearless, in stark contrast to the rest of us, during the weeks and months after the tragedy.

In trauma, the reassuring absolutisms (albeit mythical ones) of daily life—that children do not die, that worlds do not move, and that parents always survive—are replaced by other, more pernicious convictions: the "enduring, crushing meanings" (of one's aloneness, one's badness, one's taintedness, or the world's meaninglessness) that precipitate out of unbearable affect. Trauma forces one into an experience of the impersonal, random, and contingent nature of reality, but it forces one violently and against one's will. "The traumatized person cannot help but perceive aspects of existence that lie well outside the absolutized horizons of normal everydayness,"[7] says Stolorow. Trauma exposes "the unbearable embeddedness of being,"[8] in the sense that it shows us our powerlessness, our helplessness, and our inability to exist independently and *absolutely* in the way we might wish. Trauma is disillusioning, but not in the gentle way of the mother who has already given her child the illusion of omnipotence. It reveals truth, but in a manner so abrupt and disturbing that the mind jumps away. The old absolutisms no longer reassure, and the newly revealed reality feels crushing.

The Buddha managed to make trauma tolerable. He found a way of easing people into the burning nature of everything without driving them into the arms of negativity or nihilism or self-doubt or self-hate. He often used death, the very trauma that the absolutisms of daily life are designed to hold at bay, to nudge people out of their ego-centric complacency.

Yet the Buddha was not into scaring people for its own sake. He suggested that most of the time, no matter how much we think about death, we can't really understand it. The *absolutizing* tendency runs so deep that, unless death hits us over the head, we do not really appreciate its reality, even though we may mouth the words. His aim was to cut through the absolutisms of daily life, not to traumatize but to show people what he, the Buddha, had already learned. Even when he was ostensibly secure in his world of lily pools and sunshades and minstrels with no men among them and meals of rice and meat, he was delicate. Only when he was able to hold the realities of old age, illness, and death could he become strong. The effort required to ward off the possibility of trauma—the rush to normal that the absolutisms of daily life encourages—is itself traumatic.

The Buddha also used trauma to detraumatize people. Sometimes he deliberately evoked it, and sometimes he just used what people brought him. But whichever scenario he worked with, his message never varied. Facing the traumas we are made of, and the new ones that continually shape us, makes more sense than trying to avoid them, if the mind is in a balanced enough place to hold the truth. Trauma is unavoidable, despite our strong wishes to the contrary. Facing this truth, this disillusioning attack on our omnipotence, with an attitude of honesty and caring strips it of much of its threat. When we are constantly telling ourselves that things shouldn't be this way, we reinforce the very dread we are trying to get away from. But feeling our way into the ruptures of our lives lets us become more real. We begin to appreciate the fragile web in which we are all enmeshed, and we may even reach out to offer a helping hand to those who are struggling more than we are.

I had a joint session recently with a patient and her twelve-year-old daughter that made me think about this. My patient had a fight with her daughter that morning and they were both too upset to let her go to school as she was supposed to, so my patient brought her to the session. I had met her daughter once before, when she was about two years old and her babysitter was sick. My patient had brought her to a session that time, too. I remembered how verbal she was, even at that age, and how attentive her mom was to her throughout the hour in my office. Yet, ever since she was about three months old, the daughter had been inexplicably anxious. She had been dealing with it well for the past few years, but her anxiety had been cresting again lately. When her mom was out walking the dog, for instance, if she was not home at the exact moment she had said she would be home, her daughter would become completely hysterical. While she was fine at school, or on overnights with friends, at home she could be hypervigilant to the point of making her well-intentioned mother claustrophobic. The absolutisms of daily life were not working for the young girl—if her mother was late it was as if her world had crumpled completely.

I wanted to help them and did not immediately know how. But I had the feeling that the daughter did not really understand what was happening inside of her. She was seeing a cognitive-behavioral therapist, who was helping her a lot, and she had all kinds of coping strategies laid out to help manage her anxiety. There was nothing in that vein that I could offer her—she already knew much more than I did about those kinds of treatment strategies. But I knew from my own experience how excruciating it could be to wait for someone I loved. Everyone was telling her that she was overdoing it, but, as the Buddha said when he enumerated his First Noble Truth, to be separated from the loved is suffering.

"You must really miss your mom," I said. "Those are intense feelings to have." To my surprise, the ice broke. Having framed her problem as an anxiety disorder, she had not really talked much about her feelings of longing. Her basic stance was that there was something the matter with her and she had better learn to shape up. She was very sophisticated psychologically though and she liked what I said to her. "What an interesting way to put it!" she exclaimed cheerfully, her eyes brightening. It is too early to tell if this one conversation will have any lasting effect, but we had a scintillating time talking about how she could make art during those times she was most missing her mom. She was already winning poetry prizes at school. It was possible, I thought, that she could learn to bear the trauma of separation with more clarity than she had been doing, and, therefore, with less distress.

There is a famous story in the Buddhist scriptures that it is at the opposite end of the spectrum from that of my patient and her daughter but that is nevertheless related. While the scenario in my office involved the imagined threat of death erupting in the first moments of an unexplained absence, the Buddhist tale describes a sequence of actual deaths that befell one young mother in a series of tragic accidents. Together, they show the range of trauma that lurks as a real possibility for all of us: whether imagined or real. In both situations, the absolutisms of daily life were upended and intolerable emotions took center stage. And in both situations a similar therapeutic intervention was needed to deal with the "singularity" of the event. Both my patient's daughter and the heroine of the Buddhist fable felt split off from the consensual reality of other people. They were both anguished and alone and in need of a greater understanding.

The Buddhist story is of a young woman of the Buddha's time named Paṭācārā[9] (pa-*ta*-char-a) whose losses approach the limits of the imagination. The beautiful daughter of a wealthy Sāvatthī merchant,* Paṭācārā was confined to the top floor of her seven-story home when she was sixteen to prevent her from getting involved with men. Despite this measure (or perhaps because of it), she fell in love with one of her family's servants. When her parents decided to marry her off to a man of their choosing, she disguised herself as a servant girl and ran away with her lover to a faraway village, where her young husband farmed a small piece of land for them. Soon pregnant, Paṭācārā begged her spouse to take her back to her parents' home to give birth, explaining to him that her mother, seeing her with child, would forgive her and accept their union. When her husband refused, afraid that he would be arrested or killed, she set out by herself. He followed, they argued, she delivered her baby boy before she could reach her ancestral home, and, seeing no point in returning to her

---

* Sāvatthī, or Srāvastī, the capital of the kingdom of Kosala, ruled by King Pasenadi, was one of the six largest cities of India in the Buddha's time; the Buddha spent a great deal of his monastic life there, primarily at the Jetavana monastery, whose ruins can still be found.

parents once she had given birth, she returned to her adopted village with her husband.

Some time later, the sequence repeated itself. Pregnant for a second time, Paṭācārā set out for her parents' home carrying her young son. Her husband followed, caught up to her about halfway there, and tried to convince her, to no avail, to return home with him. An unexpected storm arose suddenly, lashing them with rain and frightening them with thunder and lightning, and Paṭācārā went into early labor. She asked her husband to find a place where she could give birth, and he went off to look for wood with which to build her a shelter. Chopping down some saplings, he was bitten by a poisonous snake hiding in an anthill and died. Paṭācārā gave birth alone in the midst of the storm and set out in the morning with her two children to look for her husband, discovering his corpse as she turned a bend in the road. Blaming herself for his death, she proceeded on toward Sāvatthī, and her parents' house.

On her way she came to a river swollen from the recent storm. Its waters were waist high and there was a strong current. Unable to wade across with both children in her arms, she left the older boy on one bank and ferried her baby across first. Placing him on the far bank, she returned to get her older son. Halfway back to him, she saw a hawk swoop down from the sky and pluck her baby from his resting place on the far bank. Stuck in the middle of the river, Paṭācārā could only scream as she watched the great bird fly off with the infant in its claws. Hearing her cry, her eldest son mistakenly thought she was calling for him, and he jumped into the river to try to come to her. The current was too strong for him and quickly swept him away.

But even this was not the end for Paṭācārā. More suffering awaited her. Like Kisagotami having lost her infant baby, Paṭācārā was, by now, completely traumatized. As she came to the outskirts of her parents' town, she encountered a traveler coming in the other direction. She asked if he knew her family and he reacted with alarm. "Ask me about any other family but that one," he said. The previous evening, in the sudden storm, the family's house had collapsed, killing both the elderly couple and their remaining son. "There," he said, pointing to a pale blue wisp of smoke in the distance. "If you look where I am pointing you can see the smoke from their funeral pyre." Paṭācārā's collapse was complete. "Those who saw her called her a crazy fool, threw rubbish at her, and pelted her with clods of earth, but she continued on until she reached the outskirts of Sāvatthī."[10]

The Buddha, of course, was residing nearby, surrounded by a number of disciples. He recognized her as "one who was ripe for his message of deliverance" and, against the advice of those around him who cautioned him to keep his distance from the crazy woman, he beckoned her toward him. "Sister," he cried. "Regain your mindfulness!" And, although it is not clear how she even knew what he was talking about (perhaps he said something more like "Regain your composure!"), she did. An old disciple threw his cloak around her, and she approached the Buddha to tell him of her losses.

After listening carefully, the Buddha said the following: "Paṭācārā, do not be troubled any more. You have come to one who is able to be your shelter and refuge. It is not only today that you have met with calamity and disaster, but throughout this beginningless round of existence, weeping over the loss of sons and others dear to you, you have shed more tears than the waters of the four oceans."[11]

Calmed by the Buddha's words, Paṭācārā took refuge with the community of mendicants around him. Some time later, while sitting outside and washing her feet, she noticed water trickling down the slope of a hillside. Something about the scene matched her internal experience. "Some streams sank quickly into the ground, others flowed down a little farther, while others flowed all the way to the bottom of the slope,"[12] she saw. Some were like her children, disappearing very quickly on their journey; some were like her husband, living into young adulthood; and some were like her parents, living into old age. But death was common to everyone. "Having washed my feet, I reflected upon the waters," Paṭācārā later wrote. "When I saw the foot water flow from the high ground down the slope, my mind became concentrated like an excellent thoroughbred steed."[13] Seeing her reality reflected in the natural environment awoke something in Paṭācārā. With every reason in the world to feel sorry for herself, and with the pressures of grief compressing her heart, she managed to see deeply into the nature of reality and let go of being shocked, humiliated, and disgusted. She was still sad, still grief stricken, but seeing the streams of water flowing down the hill did for her what the image of the broken glass had done for Ajahn Chah. While of course her family was precious (as was his glass), she was no longer fighting with the nature of things. Her traumas had opened her up rather than closing her off.

In exploring his own discontent, in searching for the way out of the conundrum of old age, illness, and death, the Buddha stumbled upon a pivotal truth, one that he put into practice with those, like Paṭācārā, who had suffered devastating losses, as well as with those who were doing their best to pretend that such losses could never afflict them. "You have come to one who is able to be your shelter and refuge," he told Paṭācārā. Something in their interaction, some way of relating to the tragedy with attunement and responsiveness, communicated itself to her and allowed her to hold her reality. Therapists today have come to similar conclusions. One of them, the New York psychoanalyst Michael Eigen, has described it like this: "If, for example, one's emotional reality or truth is despair, what is most important is not *that* one may be in despair, but one's attitudes *toward* one's despair. Through one's basic attentiveness one's despair can declare itself and tell its story. One enters profound dialogue with it. If one stays with this process, an evolution even in the quality of despair may begin to be perceived, since despair is never uniform."[14]

It sounds like a platitude—*despair is never uniform*—and yet there is something profound in these words. Paṭācārā was enlightened watching the rivulets of water running down the hill in front of her. Those rivulets might well have been her own tears, for all we know. Her trauma, severe as it was, was not outside the natural order of things. As the Buddha told her, trauma has been happening since the beginning of beginningless time. She may not have been able to believe in the absolutisms of daily life any longer, but her reflection on the waters freed her from the absolutism, the singularity, of her grief.

In regaining her mindfulness, as the Buddha had encouraged her to do, she found a way to relate to her pain without turning it into pathology. Entering into dialogue with it, feeling the way it ran through her, gave her a visceral feeling of the "unbearable embeddedness of being"[15] of which both she and her family were a part. She stayed with this process, and an evolution in the quality of her despair took place.

While I am afraid this story has been used over the years to caution young women against running off impetuously with their lovers, it has, for me, a much deeper purpose. Paṭācārā's pain was so intense, her losses so grievous, it was amazing that she could go on at all. I can imagine that nothing else made sense to her than to give the Buddha's counsel a chance. As Paṭācārā realized in her reflection upon the waters, there may be nothing else to do with the traumas that befall us than to use them for our own awakenings.

5

Dissociation

When the old monk who led Paṭācārā to the Buddha threw his cloak around her, he was making a vivid psychotherapeutic statement. And when the Buddha, upon hearing her story of trauma, told her that he was one who could serve as her shelter and refuge, he was putting into words what the old disciple had already tangibly displayed. Both men were suggesting that Paṭācārā's unbearable experience could be borne, if just barely. And both were addressing what is today recognized as the most common response to trauma: the tendency toward dissociation. In dissociation the personality wards off becoming fragmented. It does this by withdrawing from that which it cannot bear. The shocked self is sacrificed, sent to its room for an endless time-out. It is shunned, split off, shut away, or otherwise quieted. The unbearable nature of its ordeal is more than can be handled, more than can be processed, and certainly more than can be understood. In order to go on, the self cuts its losses and dissociates its alarm. This is a self-preserving strategy, called an "ego defense" in Western psychology, and it is one that has also been implicated in the development of posttraumatic stress. Its goal is to avoid falling apart, and it is usually marginally effective. The problem is that the dissociated aspects of the self do not go away completely. They lurk in the background, unexplored and undigested, and the ego must expend enormous energy keeping them at bay.

When the Buddha suggested that he could serve as Paṭācārā's shelter and refuge, he was speaking from experience. He had already worked through his own developmental traumas. He knew firsthand that the defense of dissociation did not have to be the last word, that it is possible to be whole even after a series of traumas. He instructed Paṭācārā in his method of mindfulness and, in so doing, gave her the antidote to dissociation. In teaching her how to release herself into her forbidden feelings, he also showed her how to emerge from them. Her reclamation of her dissociated parts can be seen not just in the image of the cloak around her shoulders but also in her connection with the physical landscape in which she was immersed. No longer needing to hold her losses at arm's length, she was able to use the waters flowing around her to connect to her own inner state. After learning to be mindfully aware, she found she did not need to sacrifice her emotional body in the pursuit of stability but could open to what Kabat-Zinn[1] has called "the full catastrophe" of her life.

Given that tales like Paṭācārā's are so central to Buddhist culture, it is surprising how little attention has been paid to the early death of the Buddha's mother. One would think that her death would figure prominently in his story because of the way it speaks to his core teachings of impermanence, indeterminacy, and suffering, but there is very little overt mention of her passing. It took me years of immersion in Buddhist thought to even become conscious of it. She is there at the beginning of the Buddha's life, exits discreetly, and is barely acknowledged thereafter. This rather curious neglect is a sign, I believe, of the traumatic underpinnings of the Buddha's biography. Even in a culture steeped in the truth of impermanence, the need to dissociate from distress is very strong. People are so eager to get on with the Buddha's journey to enlightenment that they rush right past the trauma at the heart of his early experience.

In developing the theme of an undercurrent of trauma running through the center of the Buddha's story, it is clear to me that not all Buddhists may agree. Many people are drawn to contemplative practices as a means of rising above, or distancing themselves from, their most difficult emotions. They see meditation as a way of becoming calm and clear, of removing themselves from the tumult and chaos of daily life. They are not interested in awakening their primitive agonies or being reminded of their buried losses. They see the Buddha as one who has conquered emotion, not as someone who has come to terms with it. Even the Buddha, right up until his final awakening, meditated to escape from himself. He subscribed to the dominant philosophical view of his time that the desires of the flesh bound him to an unsatisfactory existence and that liberation meant separating his consciousness from worldly preoccupations. That he eventually rejected this view is something that even devout Buddhists often do not recognize, although it was the foundation of his awakening.

From my perspective, these two phenomena—the failure of Buddhist culture to take seriously the loss at the heart of the Buddha's story and his own attempts to escape from himself—are linked. They both reflect the defense of dissociation, the very defense that the Buddha's teachings are designed to counter. In dissociation, that which is unbearable is closed off and isolated from the rest of the self. The person has to go on, but to do so he or she must turn away from trauma, compartmentalizing it in a way that keeps it out of view. In dissociation there is no self-reflection—in order to survive trauma the devastated self is immobilized and hidden out of view. The emotional impact has nowhere to go, however. It becomes stuck, in a frozen state, inaccessible to the person's usual waking consciousness. It is never digested, never symbolized or imagined, never processed by thought or language, and never really felt. As the psychologist Harvey L. Schwartz put it in a 1994 article, the mind flees its own subjectivity[2] in order to "evacuate" its pain.

Within the Buddhist literature of the past millennia, there are several references to the Buddha's loss that reflect this tendency toward dissociation. The famous myth of the baby Buddha taking seven steps to the north immediately after his birth, for example, conveniently passes over the helpless years of his infancy. These years are dissociated, as if they never existed, as if he were never a baby at all. It is as if he is already at least two or three years old, if not totally grown up, walking and talking and thinking clearly, already conscious of the role he is to play in the world at the time of his birth. His need for a mother, in this version of the story, is minimal.

In this depiction of the Buddha's infancy one can see a culture's defense mechanism at work. Rather than addressing the impact of his looming loss, the story depicts the baby as already completely self-sufficient. As much as I love the image of the baby Buddha pointing his finger in the air and trumpeting his omnipotence with what would become known as his Lion's Roar, I cannot help but wonder about the subtext of the story. It reminds me of how my own therapist (a teacher of Gestalt therapy named Isadore From) told me that he could often tell from the way his patients walked into the room who had been prodded by overeager parents into standing and walking before they were ready. The hip bones of infants are softer than those of adults and do not completely fuse for the first year of life. Parents who stand their babies up and make them imitate walking push them into an erect posture they are not physiologically ready for. The child wants to comply to please his doting parents, but such children are robbed of the satisfaction of lifting themselves to standing when their bodies are actually ready. Insecurity lurks within such a compliant personality. A sense of inner confidence is often lacking.

The Buddhist scriptures, while relatively silent on the Buddha's mother, do not completely ignore her. But when they do address her death, they illuminate the defense of dissociation more than they speak to the possible impact of her demise. Reading the various renditions of the Buddha's birth that have come down to us, one can feel that something is not being said. Everything is fine, these stories insist. Nothing to worry about. It didn't matter at all! In the description of her death in the *Lalitavistara Sutra*, for example, a Mahayana scripture written in Sanskrit and preserved in Tibetan, the pressure that must have been applied to the young Buddha to deny the depth of his loss can still be felt:

> O monks, seven days after the Boddhisattva's birth, it came time for his mother, Māyādevī, to die. And upon her death, Māyādevī was reborn into the realm of the Thirty-three gods.
>
> But monks, if you think that Māyādevī's death was due to the birth of the Boddhisattva, you are wrong. That is truly not the way to see it. And why not? Because she had reached the end of her life. With Bodhisattvas of the past also, seven days after their final birth, their mothers have died. And why? Because if a Bodhisattva were to grow up, his faculties fully developed, at the moment he left home, his mother's heart would break.[3]

This is the most common explanation for Queen Maya's death, the one that is generally repeated in Buddhist circles when her name is brought up: This is what happens to all Buddhas' mothers. In Buddhist cosmology, Buddhas arise in every age, just when the world has forgotten the last vestiges of the former one's teachings. In every case, it is said, the mother dies after the child's first week of life. Were she to live, the various commentaries assert, her heart would be broken when her son renounced his family and fled to the forest to pursue his spiritual quest. It's better, it is said, for her to die early, to be spared the unbearable pain of abandonment. It would be too cruel to subject her to such anguish.[4]

With great compassion for the mother, the various commentaries gloss over the effects on the child. It is left to the Buddha to put the pieces together himself. There is no evidence that as an infant he suffered in any material way from his mother's sudden death. Nor was there any hint of neglect or abuse on the part of the aunt toward her nephew. One can only imagine that the young child took her for his own mother and bonded with her as such. It is likely that the infant, while having lost the opportunity to feed from his own mother's breast, would have been fed by well-practiced wet nurses and doted on by the extended family of the Sakya clan, and it is even possible, had his mother lived, that his feedings would have been the responsibility of the same relatives or servants. He was certainly not in the classic position of an orphaned baby left alone in a less-than-optimal institutional setting, nor was he like the son of the poet Sylvia Plath, one year old at the time of his mother's suicide, whose father, Ted Hughes, perhaps anticipating the boy's own suicide forty-six years later, wrote of how his eyes "became wet jewels/The hardest substance of the purest pain/ As I fed him in his high white chair."[5]

But the Buddha, we can infer from his own remembrances, did not escape entirely unaffected. "I was delicate, most delicate, supremely delicate," he recounted, without saying, and without necessarily knowing, why. He was "shocked, humiliated and disgusted" when confronted with old age, sickness, and death, and he was under intense pressure from his family to keep all three at arm's length throughout his first twenty-nine years of life. Unsettled by the forces that whisked away his mother, he and his family dealt with the trauma of her loss in the usual way. They dissociated the pain, allowing themselves to go on, but in a compromised state. The Buddha's delicacy speaks to this compromise. Without language for illness and death, with the whole thing cut out of his experience, there was a fragility in him that reflects the effort involved in keeping such an intense event away from his consciousness. As he himself reported, when he was exposed, as if for the first time, to the instability underlying his life, he suddenly realized he was "not safe."

A hint of the Buddha's dissociation comes in one of the verses of the first literary biography of the Buddha, the *Buddhacarita*, an epic Indian poem of the first century CE by Ashva·ghosha, whose title means "Life of the Buddha." Written in Sanskrit by a learned scholar who had converted to Buddhism, *Buddhacarita* wove the facts of the Buddha's life—his birth, awakening, philosophy, and death—into a lyrical celebration of his teachings directed at the cultural and literary establishment of the day, to whom the Buddha's teachings, six hundred years after his death, were still something of a novelty. In this particular verse, the young Gotama exclaims in horror at his first glimpse of old age on his second trip outside the palace. Here he can be heard describing the ravaged soul he has just seen:

> His belly swollen, his body heaves as he pants;
> his arms and shoulders droop,
> his limbs are thin and pale;
> Leaning on someone, he cries "Mother!" piteously;
> tell me, who is this man?[6]

In some way, of course, at least metaphorically, the Buddha must have been peering at his own reflection. The old, sick man crying for his mother might just be a disguised version of his week-old self, weeping inconsolably for his suddenly departed mother. Belly swollen, body heaving, arms and shoulders drooping, limbs thin and pale; the description certainly fits a bereft child as much as it does a sickly old man. And Gotama's puzzlement at the sight has all of the hallmarks of a contemporary therapy patient struggling to make sense of a split-off aspect of his own self. Teetering precariously at the edge of his seat, such a patient, estranged from his emotional self, is likely to feel a bit confused when his true feelings start to dawn.

"Tell me," said Gotama while staring at this vision of himself, "who is this man?" That is the question that came to preoccupy him over the next six years. Having woken up to the reality of death, sorrow, and loss; having seen his delicate nature; having a beginning inkling of the dissociated remnant of primitive agony lurking within, Gotama was poised to confront the harsh truths of existence, truths that, for him, included the inexplicable absence at the heart of his early life.

We now use words like "estrangement" and "dissociation" to describe the coping mechanisms people use to deal with trauma. But in the Buddha's time such concepts could only be inferred. And although it has not often been recognized or acknowledged, the psychological teachings of the Buddha do suggest this phenomenon. For in order to become a Buddha, Gotama had to remember what he had never entirely understood and reexperience what he had only temporarily known. His task was different from Paṭācārā's. Her losses occurred when she was an adult, and she could summon both her love and her grief when it became safe enough to do so. His loss occurred in an infantile and preverbal state. He had no way to remember his mother and no way to process his loss. And yet, before he could complete his journey, the trauma that configured his self had to be brought into awareness, experienced as if for the first time, and transfigured. The split that the young Gotama endured needed to be healed. The Buddha had to invent a therapy for himself and apply it. As one of today's leading experts on developmental trauma, Philip Bromberg, has put it, "No matter how great the pain of being trapped within one's internal object world, and no matter how desperate the wish to break free, it is humanly impossible to become fully alive in the present without facing and owning all of the hated, disavowed parts of the self that have shaped and been shaped by one's earliest object attachments."[7]

For some reason, therapists writing about early intimate relationships between infants and caregivers like to speak of "objects" instead of "people." The idea, I believe, is that babies are incapable of relating to whole persons, that they relate, instead, to objects (like the breast) or functions (like feeding, holding, or soothing). They become attached to these objects or functions or traumatized by the lack of them. If they are hungry, for instance, they do not yet know they are hungry; they are moved by a physiological and biological urge to cry out. It is up to the parents, the "objects" of the baby's subjective experience, to respond to the baby's cry. When a therapist writes about being "trapped in one's internal object world," he is writing about being trapped by primitive agonies, about the constraints dissociated traumas put on the mind. While the Buddha's story is traditionally related in metaphorical, not psychological, language, a careful examination of it reveals a similar psychological process underlying it. Just as described above, the Buddha could become "fully alive in the present" only by engaging with the "hated, disavowed parts of the self" that were configured by his earliest relationships. He found a method of dealing with dissociation before there was even a concept of it. In so doing, he not only awoke to his own Buddha nature but also came to understand it as a reflection of his lost mother.

Therapists today have a language for trauma's impact on the

mind. They recognize that the mind's primary defense against agony is dissociation and that the primary motivation for dissociation is stability. Especially in situations in which unbearable emotions are stirred up, the self's only choice is to wall itself off from whatever is threatening it, to remove itself from what it cannot regulate. My friend whose parents were both alcoholics with violent tempers became a person who was always most eager to please. Her parents used to have terrible arguments, smashing furniture while she cowered with her siblings under the bed. Yet she showed not a trace of her anger or fear to anyone as she moved into her adulthood. She was ultracapable but suffered, in her thirties, from what seemed to her to be irrational bouts of intense anxiety about her children's safety and well-being. This capacity for dissociation is a survival mechanism. It allows us to go forward with our lives but in a compromised condition. The shock of trauma sits outside awareness like a coiled spring. The emotions aroused—which by their very "unbearable" nature cannot be imagined—are left unexplored. The self that moves forward is restricted by its failure to integrate the traumatic impact, by its failure to process its unbearable feelings. In its attempts to "ensure that what has already happened is unlikely ever to be repeated in the same way,"[8] the defense of dissociation splits the self into a fiefdom of incompatible states. "The price for this protection," says Bromberg, "is to plunder future personality development of its resiliency and render it into a fiercely protected constellation of relatively unbridgeable self-states, each rigidly holding its own truth and its own reality 'on call,' ready to come 'on stage' as needed, but immune to the potentially valuable input from other aspects of self."[9] One of the consequences of this defense is that the self is depleted of emotional depth and fluidity. "Dissociation shows its signature not by disavowing aspects of mental *contents* per se, but through the patient's alienation from aspects of *self* that are inconsistent with his experience of 'me' at a given moment. It functions because conflict is *unbearable* to the mind, not because it is *unpleasant*."[10]

In the second chapter of Ashva·ghosha's *Buddhacarita* there is a single verse about the demise of the future Buddha's mother that speaks directly to the defense of dissociation. Written in Sanskrit, the verse was recently translated as follows:

> But when queen Maya saw the immense might
> of her son, like that of a seer divine,
> she could not bear the delight it caused her;
> so she departed to dwell in heaven.[11]

I was startled when I first came upon this verse. "The immense might" of the infant! His mother's inability to "bear the delight it caused her"! The verse seemed to support Winnicott's descriptions of the merciless way an infant loves his mother, the way he beats her like a drum with a mix of what we in hindsight would call need, hunger, love, aggression, and entitlement but that in an infant comes all in one package, undifferentiated, like a force of nature. As Winnicott explained in an early paper, "The normal child enjoys a ruthless relation to his mother, mostly showing in play, and he needs his mother because only she can be expected to tolerate his ruthless relation to her even in play, because this really hurts her and wears her out. Without this play with her he can only hide a ruthless self and give it life in a state of dissociation."[12]

The translation of the Buddhist verse hints at a very similar psychodynamic. What kind of message did the infant Buddha receive from Maya when she died? Did he need to hide his ruthless self in deference to his mother's reaction? Was this what his father covertly demanded of him by structuring his subsequent life to have no reference to old age, illness, or death? Is this what made him feel so delicate? If Winnicott's musings apply, in what later state of dissociation would he have been able to give life back to his ruthless self? As we shall see, there is evidence to suggest that his six years in the forest after leaving home provided him ample opportunity to dwell within just the sort of dissociated state Winnicott envisioned.

I was moved, however, not only by the thought of the infant Buddha without his mother to absorb his love but also by the image of a mother unable to bear her delight. Having fathered two children myself, I felt a vague sympathy for Maya. In psychoanalysis these days, the emphasis is so often on the psychic state of the infant that the intensity of adult experience is commonly shortchanged. And it seems easier for psychoanalysts to talk about negative feelings—aggression and its derivatives—than about ordinary ecstatic ones that evoke fear as well as pleasure. The delight of the parent seems a wonderful thing to highlight.

Ashva·ghosha's biography actually makes another reference to the Buddha's parents' delight, in its first chapter, when describing their reactions to his birth. Both parents can be seen trying to contain a mix of hope and dread, as if anticipating Maya's capitulation a week later.

> When he saw the wondrous birth of his son,
> the king, although steadfast, was much perturbed;
> and from his love two streams of tears surged forth,
> rising from apprehension and delight.

> The queen was overcome with fear and joy,
> like a mixed stream of water, hot and cold;
> both because her son's power was other than human,
> and because of a mother's natural weakness.[13]

The idea of the Buddha's parents having a hard time with the feelings evoked by their baby moved me because it hinted at a truth I never could have articulated but that fit with my experience. Love enlivens but also frightens, not only when it falters or when it is unrequited but also when it is unleashed, dissolving us in the heat of its expression. It takes stamina and faith to maintain oneself in the midst of such passion. Maya was not the first, nor the last, to retreat from it, to question her ability to survive its intensity.

Within the psychoanalytic tradition, it was Winnicott who first paid attention to this dimension of the mother–infant relationship. He looked at it through the lens of breast-feeding, which at the time was under assault by the medicalization and mechanization of childrearing. It took Winnicott to remind therapists—and parents—how meaningful nursing can be for a mother. With care to avoid presuming that it was right for everyone or every situation, and with barely concealed horror at those who would "make" mothers breast-feed, Winnicott nevertheless took care to repeatedly affirm its primal power at a time (in the early 1960s) when the medical establishment was counseling just the opposite.

> Alongside the observation of the baby's experiences which are richer when the breast is being used than with a bottle, one has to put all that the mother herself feels and experiences. I prefer to leave it to your imagination, but it is important to draw attention to the fact that although the feeding of a baby can be very satisfactory, however it is done, the satisfaction is of a different order altogether for the woman who is able to use part of her own body in this way. The satisfaction links up with her own experiences when she was a baby, and the whole thing goes back to the beginning of time when human be-

ings had scarcely moved from the position of mammalian animal life.[14]

There is something in the nursing experience that connects a woman not only to her infant but to her selfless self. The Sanskrit verse says much the same thing. Maya felt the vast luster of her connection with her child but did not think she could sustain the thrill of bliss it brought her. The feelings evoked, although positive, were unbearable, and her only solution was to dissociate herself from them. She left her physical body behind and retreated to the only place that felt safe enough to sustain the thrill of bliss she could not otherwise process: a heaven realm where, according to Buddhist cosmology, beings have bodies of bliss rather than flesh and blood. Her son, meanwhile, was left to work things out for himself.

From a trauma perspective, Queen Maya's death had to impact her child, even if the care he received from her surrogates turned out to be loving and tender. There could be no way to entirely paper over the cut. At the beginning of life, as Winnicott once put it, it "seems impossible to talk about the individual without talking about the mother."[15] While an infant already has the potential for separateness, he is in a state of absolute dependency such that the mother's relating cannot be discriminated from the baby's own self. "How the mother behaves is really part of the infant," Winnicott surmised. "I think the difficulty is that there's a paradox. The paradox is that the environment is part of the infant and at the same time it isn't. The infant has to accept this eventually in order to become a grown-up at all."[16]

If how the mother behaves is really part of the infant, then the young boy who was to become the Buddha had to make sense out of something quite confusing. At the very beginning of his life, a tremendous disruption took place, a disruption for which there could have been no words. And if the silence about Queen Maya's death that has come to characterize Asian culture was present in the Buddha's day as well, it is likely that there were never words about it, even as the child matured. Having been let down, the young Buddha was given a very early, if momentary, taste of aloneness. His mother's disappearance would have become part of him, and while it would be premature to assume that he took her abandonment personally (since there was very little of a person present yet to take it that way), it is fair to wonder whether his personality would have been conditioned by his mother's sudden absence. Her inability to sustain the thrill of bliss he brought her would have stayed with him, in one form or another.

Maya's predicament mirrored one that the Buddha would confront over and over again in his adult years. People could not believe in their own Buddha nature. Even Gotama himself, in his preenlightenment years, could not believe in his inherent perfection. He thought he had to extinguish himself to find transcendence. His mother acted out of a similar belief. Unable to stay with the thrill in her human embodiment, unable to believe that her physical body could bear her joy, Maya was forced to take refuge in her celestial bliss body, the only one that could hold the feelings evoked by her child. In so doing, the Buddha's mother acted out an inadequacy that many a mother—like many a lover—is vulnerable to, an inadequacy fed by thoughts of doubt and fear that erode confidence and corrode connection. Doubting the capacity of her physical form to sustain the thrill of her motherhood, Maya was compelled to seek a self-state that split her off from her child. Like an infant forced to disconnect from his ruthless self when his mother fails to receive it, Maya could endure only by dissociating. Forsaking her body and her child, she survived by departing her physical form.

While the main Buddhist commentaries emphasize Maya's altruism in bearing the infant Gotama and then fulfilling her preordained role as a future Buddha's mother by dying when she was supposed to, this other dynamic deepens her connection to the Buddha's awakening. Many years later, after a six-year struggle and one of the world's great self-analyses, the Buddha attained his enlightenment. Although he has become known for his proclamation of the universality of suffering, the Buddha's most radical statement was not about suffering at all; it was about joy. The actual nature of life is bliss, the Buddha said, but this bliss is too often obscured by our habitual misperceptions. It is the egocentric life that is suffering, the Buddha realized, the life conditioned by conceit that needs a self to be built up and protected and separated out, in its own version of dissociation, from the rest of the universe. The Buddha's discovery was not of suffering but of freedom. He did not need to discover suffering: Its existence was already obvious to everyone. What the Buddha found was that suffering was not irredeemable, that it is dependent, not only on the way things are but on the way we think and react. In uncovering the defense of dissociation, the Buddha spoke to his own mother's dilemma, to the conundrum or conflict that his birth had forced on her but that she was unable to process. The thrill of bliss *can* be sustained in a human body, he proclaimed, once this bliss is understood as an expression of the compassionate connection that binds us all the way a mother is naturally connected to her baby.

No one doubts, as today's therapists like to remind people, that mothers suffer. But mothers (and fathers, too), through their identifications with their babies, do not ordinarily let their suffering be the last word. Love lifts them out of self-preoccupation and connects them to a joy greater than that obtainable through the satisfaction of egocentric desires. The Buddha's mother glimpsed this truth but, to fulfill her function as the mother of a future Buddha, she worried about her ability to sustain it. The Buddha, in his awakening, saw the potential for boundless compassion inherent in everyone and realized that it need not make us afraid. Early in his teaching career, during the three-month period of the Indian summer monsoon, the Buddha, according to legend, traveled to the heaven realm where his mother had taken refuge to acknowledge the truth of the bliss she had felt when he was born. He taught her the basics of his psychology, as if to enlighten her about her own true nature. He had an obligation to the mother who had borne him and a rupture to repair. Having discovered his own bliss body, he needed to reassure his mother that he had not forgotten hers.

I was thinking about this not long ago when teaching a weekend workshop on Buddhism and psychotherapy in New York City, where I live. It was a workshop in which I tried to balance talk with silent meditation so people could get a glimpse of how mindfulness actually works to counter the defense of dissociation. I led off the morning session with a meditation on sound. I asked everyone to take out their cell phones and turn them on, preferably with a favorite ringtone, so that the phones would make noise when they went off. My idea was to counter the usual notions of meditation as demanding silence and to encourage an attitude of openness to all experience, even that which can feel unbearable. I was trying to show how meditation can be therapeutic, how it teaches a nonjudgmental way of attending to thoughts and feelings, and how listening to sounds can be practice for listening to feelings.

I liked the idea of the cell phones going off randomly in the midst of our group meditation as people got calls, voice messages, e-mails, and texts. I saw the resulting cacophony as a metaphor not only for the traumas of daily life but also for its emotional impact as well: unpredictable, chaotic, inconvenient, and emerging in its own way and on its own schedule. Many people have the idea that meditation means shutting down thought or shutting off emotions the way we are often asked to shut down our phones before a movie or a talk. I wanted to use the ubiquitous presence of sound as an object of meditation rather than seeing it as an unwanted disturbance. By inference I was suggesting that emotional life could be part of the meditative experience, not something reserved for one's diary, one's partner, or one's therapy and not something to be ashamed of or to squelch in the hopes of a more "spiritual" experience. I enjoyed seeing people's surprise when I first suggested the exercise. Their nervous laughter gladdened my therapist heart.

"You'll see," I said encouragingly. "You're not as popular as you might think. Who's going to be calling you on a Saturday morning anyway? We'll still have plenty of silence in the room." I asked the participants to use the sounds that did come as reminders to pay attention, the way Zen meditators might use the striking of a stick on the shoulders as a means of staying alert. I asked everyone to make the exercise a meditation on hearing, and I quoted Freud giving recommendations to physicians practicing psychoanalysis. He had one important secret for therapists. "Simply listen," Freud suggested, "and don't bother about keeping anything in mind." I told them how Freud's daughter, Anna, had said that the therapist sits in the center of an equilateral triangle, equidistant from id, ego, and superego, consciously not aligning herself with any aspect of her patient's psyche. In meditation, we similarly sit without judgment, equidistant from instinct, ego, and self-criticism.

The meditation proceeded without a hitch. There was an intermittent low swishing sound that seemed to come from the ventilation system, a whooshing noise that was gently soothing and easy to attend to. People shifted in their chairs and coughed occasionally while random noises filtered in from the street. And once in a while someone's phone would go off, a sudden burst of fireworks: a bit of Motown, a flurry of salsa, little musical explosions piercing the room's relative silence. The zings and zats of sound lent an electrical charge to the meditation, sparkling like slivers of stars in the stillness that settled over the group as we sat.

After the meditation there was time for questions. The third or fourth person to raise a hand was a young Hispanic woman who seemed reluctant to speak, even as she waited her turn. But when she began, she captured everyone's attention. "My father died several months ago," she began. Her voice quavered but grew stronger as she continued. "He was sick for about a year before he died. I helped to take care of him—I had a special ring in my phone for him so I would know when he was calling me. But since he died, I haven't been able to look at certain things that remind me of him, or listen to things, like his voice on the answering machine. I put his ringtone away; I would never use it for anyone else, and I couldn't bear to hear it anymore. But in this group, someone else had the same tone, the one I had saved for my father. And when it went off while we were sitting, it was like my father calling to me again—it brought him back. I felt so lucky to be hearing it now, for the first time after his death, in this room, with all of you. I was afraid to face it, but I felt as if everyone was supporting me while I listened. I was scared of what I would feel, but it was good."

I have never seen this woman again but her response, or the spirit behind her response, has stayed with me. It was much more moving than I am capable of conveying on the page. Her love for her father came shining through for everyone to see. The meditation, in inadvertently summoning him, had reached deep inside her heart and released its sweetness. By chance, it had brought her father back, opening her once again to the sound of him.

I was struck by how readily our meditation had plucked a relational chord. I had wanted, by focusing on sound as the object of meditation, to help people see that meditation was not just about seeking inner peace, it was about being present with everything. To witness the release of a dissociative defense in the midst of the sound meditation was a very powerful experience. We could literally feel the young woman's self open up as she brought back her love for her father. The flow of feeling, like the rivulets of water that Paṭācārā saw as she washed her feet after meeting the Buddha, ran through the entire group of people in the room.

This was not an anomaly. There is support for it going all the way back to the Pali Canon. The collection of verses in which the Buddha tells the story of his mother's death is called *Udana*, which means "cries" or "sighs" of the heart. The reference is to the throat chakra, or center, of classical Indian spiritual anatomy, which, when a person is overwhelmed with joy or rapture, fills to overflow and erupts with song. It is intriguing that the only classical reference to the Buddha's early loss comes in this particular volume.

"Shortlived are the mothers of Bodhisattvas," the Buddha is heard to remark, referring to himself as a Bodhisattva, or awakened being.

"When the Bodhisattvas are seven days born, their mothers make an end and are reborn in the company of the Tusita devas."[17]*

The Buddha then goes on to give a little inspiration. Everyone faces impermanence, he says. All that comes into being shall eventually depart. There is no absolute safety. Seeing this fact, wise people seek liberation. This is what we would expect him to say. But there is another layer of meaning in his verse as well, one that the young woman's response to the cell-phone meditation also conveyed. When the dissociative reaction to trauma is relaxed and the self can open to what has previously seemed unbearable, a cry or sigh of release comes forth. By placing his only acknowledgment of his mother's death in the chapter called *Udana*, the Buddha pointed to an important psychological

---

* One of the highest god realms of the Buddhist cosmology.

truth. While dissociation offers immediate protection from the traumas of life, its relaxation connects us to ourselves in a way that brings forth relief from the heart. While the random ringing of the cell phone unexpectedly performed this function in my workshop, the Buddha would not have been surprised. The method he cultivated, of listening unapologetically to the sound of all things, was precisely calibrated to render the defense of dissociation mute. When this happens, the thrill of bliss that so paralyzed his mother can once again be felt.

6

Curiosity

The Buddha was very smart about the mind. Psychiatrists and brain scientists today are just catching up to him. He knew that the mind is not a monolithic entity, that it is not one thing, and that it is capable of incredible plasticity. He could see that it is adept at multiple perspectives, that it can think and be aware of its thinking at the same time. He also understood that the mind's capacity for self-reflection is the key to finding its way out of trauma. Despite his reputed, but only occasionally manifested, psychic powers, he was not a faith healer and he could not free anyone through the laying on of his hands. But he *was* a teacher, and once he figured out his method he gave it away freely, adapting it to suit the needs of the individuals he came in contact with. When I taught the meditation on sound to the participants at my weekend workshop and had people open to the ringing of their cell phones, I was trying to introduce them to his method. By listening meditatively, we were changing the way we listen, pulling ourselves out of our usual orientation to the world based on our likes and dislikes. Rather than trying to figure out what was going on around us, resisting the unpleasant noises and gravitating toward the mellifluous ones, we were listening in a simpler and more open manner. We had to find and establish another point of reference to listen in this way, one that was outside the ego's usual territory of control. You might say we were simply listening, but it was actually more complex than that. While listening, we were also aware of ourselves listening, and at the same time we were conscious of what the listening evoked within. Unhooked from our usual preoccupations, we were listening from a neutral place. For the young woman whose father had just died, this exercise, of listening in another way, turned out to be healing.

In the practice of mindfulness, the ego's usual insistence on control and security is deliberately and progressively undermined. This is accomplished by steadily shifting one's center of gravity from the thinking mind to a neutral object like the breath, or in the case of my workshop, the random sounds of the environment. As therapists who have worked with dissociation can testify, the self's primary preoccupation in response to trauma is to protect itself from being overwhelmed or hurt. The effort to maintain cohesion, to avoid fragmentation and distress, is centered in the thinking mind. The ego takes charge, banishes that which is threatening, and carries on in a limited, reduced, or constrained state. The self we ordinarily identify with, the ego, is the caretaker trying to maintain control. Other aspects of the self, including the unbearable feelings evoked by one's traumas, are relegated to the periphery, often outside conscious awareness. We think of this coping mechanism as a rational process—it certainly employs the machinery of rational thought—but therapists have come to agree with the Buddha that the overinsistence on self-control is severely limiting and ultimately irrational because of the way it excludes feeling.

In mindfulness meditation, the self that needs protection is put into neutral. The observing self slips into the space between the ego and the dissociated aspects of the personality and observes from there.

The breath, or sound, becomes the central object of focus, as opposed to thought. Thinking becomes one more thing to observe in the field of awareness but is robbed of its preeminent position. Do not grasp after the pleasant or push away the unpleasant, but give equal attention to everything there is to observe, taught the Buddha. This is difficult at first but becomes remarkably easy once one gets the hang of it. One learns first to bring one's attention to the neutral object and then to relax into a state of choiceless awareness rather than always trying to maintain control. As the ego's position is weakened, waking life takes on aspects of dream life to the extent that new surprises keep unexpectedly emerging. In the cell-phone meditation, the surprise for the woman I have described was her father's ringtone, redolent with personal meaning. But there are many other such surprises.

There is no single word for meditation in the original language of Buddhism. The closest is one that translates as "mental development." Meditation, as taught by the Buddha, is a means of investigating the mind by bringing the entire range of thoughts, feelings, and physical sensations into awareness. This not only makes what we would today call "the unconscious" conscious but also makes the conscious more conscious. There were already various forms of meditation widely practiced in the Buddha's day, but they were all techniques that solely emphasized concentration. The Buddha, before his awakening, mastered each of them but still felt uneasy. It was fine to rest the mind on a single object: a sound (like a mantra), an image (like a candle flame), a feeling (like love or compassion), or an idea. This gave strength to the mind, a feeling of stability, of peace and tranquility, a sense of what Freud, knowing just a little about Eastern philosophy, came to call the "oceanic feeling." While this could be relaxing, it did not free the mind from the traumas that had conditioned it. The Buddha was after something more.

The meditation that the Buddha found most helpful was moment-to-moment awareness of what is actually happening at successive moments of perception. This did not mean resting the mind on a single object but meant observing the mind in action from a neutral place. Human beings have the peculiar ability to be self-reflective, to witness themselves even as they are in process. The Buddha's method harnessed this ability and developed it. Tibetan Buddhists describe this kind of meditation as setting up a spy-consciousness in the corner of the mind, eavesdropping on whatever is going on. Freud described something similar when he invited psychoanalysts to "suspend judgment and give impartial attention to everything there is to observe." People are surprised to find that the mind, when subjected to this kind of self-awareness, reveals all kinds of secrets. The Buddha called this form of mental development "mindfulness" and suggested the breath as a starting point. Watching the breath trains you to watch the mind, to observe the flow instead of reacting to it. It is the cloak that Buddha's disciple threw over the devastated Paṭācārā after the death of her entire family and it is the shelter the Buddha offered to everyone. Clinicians from many schools of psychotherapy have discovered mindfulness and have begun teaching it as a method of stress relief and as an adjunct to therapy. Brain scientists have shown that areas of the brain associated with self-awareness and compassion grow in response to it.

To experience a taste of this, try sitting quietly in an upright posture. It could be in a chair or on the sofa or cross-legged on the floor. Keep your back straight. Or lie down if you would rather. Let your eyes gently close. And just listen. Listen to the sounds and the silence that surround you. Let the sounds come and go as they may without choosing one over another. Try to listen to the entire sound, noticing when your mind identifies it as whatever it is: a car horn, the refrigerator, the heat coming on, children's voices, the dog, or nothing. Don't let your identification of the sound stop you from listening. Simply note the thought and return to the bare sounds, to the act of listening. If your mind wanders, as it will, bring your attention back to the sounds. It might be after a moment or two, or it might be after a whole cascade of thoughts; it doesn't matter. At some point you will realize, "Oh, I'm not listening, I'm thinking," and at that point you can return attention to the sounds. Treat your mind the way you would a young child who doesn't know any better. Be gentle but firm. Meditation means bringing your mind back when you notice it has wandered; it's not about keeping your mind from wandering in the first place. You will notice that you instinctively prefer some sounds over others—don't let this influence your listening. Observe the liking or the not liking, but don't let it control you. Listen to everything, the way you would listen to music.

After five minutes, or ten, or fifteen—it doesn't matter—open your eyes and resume your day. For a moment or two things might seem more alive.

This is the first step, but it is not the whole meditative process. Mindfulness, in its fullest flowering, actually balances two distinct mental qualities: relaxation and investigation. In the above exercise, the relaxing aspect is in the lead and is creating the possibility for investigation. Settling into the sounds drops us into a space between our thinking mind and all that we are dissociated from. The self shifts into neutral, but we do not go blank. We are still there, more aligned with the breath or the sounds than with our discursive mind and able to observe from a new place. This "dropping back" or "settling in" is an accomplishment, and it often feels like a surprise. I always assumed that whoever it was that was doing the thinking inside my head was the real me. When I shifted my awareness in meditation, so that I was observing my thoughts instead of being run by them, it felt like a revelation.

When the Buddha compared mindfulness to both the impartiality of someone observing from on high and the penetration of a surgeon's probe, he was highlighting its double-edged nature. It encourages both detachment *and* investigation; release into a neutral space and critical inquiry when one is there. It has both passive and active qualities. Mindfulness does not mean stewing in one's own juices or merely accepting what is. A recently deceased American Zen master and navy veteran, John Daido Loori, used to say that those who think Buddhism is just about stillness end up sitting very silently up to their necks in their own shit. The active and investigative dimension of mindfulness opposes this tendency. It encourages one to examine the strangeness of one's own internal landscape from a neutral perspective. No longer being exclusively identified with the ego's need for structure and stability, no longer being driven by the "face" one puts on for the world (or for oneself), creates the possibility of releasing oneself from old habits that have become ingrained in the personality.

I was reminded of this not long ago while on my way to a week-long silent retreat in rural Massachusetts. The retreat is an opportunity to practice mindfulness uninterruptedly, to allow it to gather force when one is free from the distractions and responsibilities of ordinary life. It is a chance to dwell in the neutral space that mindfulness makes available for a prolonged period of time and to see what happens. I have been to a lot of these retreats, and I always look forward to them with a mix of hope and dread. The experience can be delightful, but it can also be tedious or excruciating, and it is often a challenging mix of all three. It is, above all else, entirely unpredictable.

Before checking in to the retreat, I stopped by to visit with Joseph Goldstein, who lives nearby. Joseph is the Buddhist teacher whom I have studied with for the longest time. He founded the retreat center where I was going to meditate, and he is a real expert on the ins and outs of intensive meditation. I have known him since I was twenty years old and first became drawn to meditation, and I consider him to be a kind of mentor.

"Everyone's asking me if I'm excited to be going on retreat," I told him. "'Excited' doesn't seem like the best word," I added, thinking of the countless hours of silent sitting and walking I had in front of me, "but I couldn't quite come up with the right adjective. 'Relieved' didn't seem quite right, either."

"How about 'curious'?" Joseph responded.

I was struck by his reply. Despite years of experience with these retreats, 'curious' would not have been a word I would have come up with on my own. Like many people drawn to the Buddhist world, I am probably too attached to the relaxation that meditation sometimes offers and driven to these retreats by an underlying hope for a transcendental experience. When the retreats turn out to be more of a struggle, I sometimes feel cheated or defeated, as if the only real point of them were to vacation in a heaven realm. I was glad to have had this brief conversation with Joseph before this particular retreat. It helped prepare me for what I was about to encounter.

On the second night of the retreat, I awoke suddenly at three thirty in the morning with a burst of anxiety. I remember being upset with myself that I wasn't sleeping through the night. I don't know what woke me up—some kind of tension in my sleep, probably, a dream I could not recall—but suddenly, there I was. Awake. After a day or two of meditation I was expecting to be calmed down and sleeping through the night, not waking up and feeling stressed out, but there was nothing to do about it. Taking Ambien on a meditation retreat didn't make any sense. I resigned myself to being up and dragged myself to a sitting position. Wide eyed in the middle of the cold February night, I wrapped myself in a blanket and positioned myself on my cushion. I did my best to remain mindful. When I lay back down after about an hour, I dreamed the following dream.

I was driving home with my wife in a car that was filled with stuff: a new computer or iPad, bunches of suitcases, a stroller, and boxes of art supplies. My wife got out of the car, fell, got up, and walked away in the direction of home. I pulled over, began to unpack the car, took out the stroller, pulled my sweater off over my head, looked back, and saw that the car was gone. A familiar phrase ran through my head as I scanned the horizon for my automobile: "unable to find what I was formerly sure was there." I remember chuckling to myself in my dream, almost as if I were aware I was dreaming, even while I was filled with trepidation at the loss of my car and all my belongings. That phrase is a Buddhist phrase. It refers to the experience in meditation when the self that one was formerly sure was there becomes impossible to locate. The feeling of not being able to find the presumed self is said to be a vertiginous one, and the feeling in the dream bore this out. It was a confusing sensation. I called my wife, got no answer, and then called the police. They put me on hold and I walked home, scared to tell my wife what I had lost. "Prepare yourself," I told her. But she was not upset. Relieved, I walked with her across an athletic field. People were playing boules on the lawn. One ball came flying toward my head; I ducked to avoid it and woke up with my heart racing. Once again. Now it was six in the morning.

I remembered my conversation with Joseph when I woke from my dream, my heart pounding from my most recent narrow escape. This was not what I had had in mind when I signed up for the retreat. I had wanted a good night's sleep, at the very least. And I was still hoping, in my heart of hearts, for a quick infusion of relaxation from all this meditation. I felt chagrined at the level of distress I was subject to, and I had to struggle to bring Joseph's words back to my mind. But as I continued to have more and more active dreams throughout the week, each of which I remembered vividly upon awakening, the wisdom of his comment became clear. Mindfulness was making it possible for me to observe my dreaming self in a manner not ordinarily available to me. In my regular life, I might be having similar dreams—filled with dissociative elements—but I would forget them immediately upon awakening in my return to everyday life. In the retreat, with so little going on in my outside world, there was tremendous opportunity to explore my inner world. While my days became relatively calm and peaceful, at night, in my sleep, I was racing through a European countryside in a car with no brakes, making 180 degree screeching turns at sixty miles an hour to bring myself to a halt. Whatever else I thought I was doing on my meditation retreat, in my unconscious I was definitely grappling with my anxiety.

Michael Eigen, a psychoanalyst whose work I have already quoted several times, is an expert on dreams. His reflections, which I read months after my retreat, helped me understand what was happening as mindfulness gained strength and my defenses relaxed. "The Talmud says every dream is an unopened letter from God,"[1] he writes. "We don't open, or are unable to open, too many of these letters. But sometimes a letter haunts us." Dreams are a way of revealing and deepening emotional experience, he conjectures, a means of emotional digestion. "The core of the dream is not the manifest content but the emotional experience." Dreams show us things about ourselves we wish to forget and at the same time help us to forget the things we can't help but remember. They are a means of holding, and sometimes processing or even resolving, traumatic experiences. As Eigen writes,

> Most dreams are aborted. Aborted experience. Something happens to frustrate the dream. An arc of experience falls short, is broken off before completion. Perhaps the dream is attempting to portray something broken, interrupted, incomplete, fragmented. Perhaps the very experience of incompletion and interruption is being dramatized and fed to us. As if the feeling of something being aborted is part of our insides. An intimation of aborted lives or aborted feelings. Something happens that doesn't go all the way, doesn't reach absolute

fulfillment. A dream breaks off and we have a sense of aborted experiencing. Broken dreams, expressing broken aspects of our beings.[2]

This idea, of broken dreams expressing broken aspects of our beings, seems very apropos. It is another way of talking about the trauma of everyday life, about the bits and pieces of catastrophe we dissociate from but still carry with us. These traumatic experiences are left hanging just outside awareness. They peek out from our dreams or nag at us in the privacy of our aloneness, a lurking sense of sorrow or disquiet that underlies our attempts to be "normal," but it is rare that we feel secure enough to let them fully speak. While I might have preferred to have my retreat be filled with pleasant feeling, this was not the path the Buddha had in mind when he laid out his teachings. My work in the retreat was, in the spirit of curiosity, to make room for the entire range of my emotional experience, to allow the dreams to be dreamed, the feelings to be felt, and my pride to be wounded.

Michael Eigen, in his discussion of broken dreams, maintains that these unwanted aspects of ourselves are in what he calls "constant conjunction" with the acceptable, that the "angry God" and the "benevolent God" are both active in us. Relief comes, in part, when we stop fending off the unpleasant and allow it to be an equal part of our experience. "Our job with our patients and with ourselves is to help make room for this sequence, for this inner rhythm, for different transformations of this constant conjunction. Not to get rid of it. We cannot get rid of it. We'd be getting rid of ourselves. Even in nirvana, you will not get rid of it. One has to learn to live with it, have a larger frame of reference, open the playing field, make more room."[3] While I thought I knew this already, both theoretically and experientially, I was, nevertheless, taken aback by the intensity of the anxiety in my retreat dreams. "No rest for the weary," I told myself after the third or fourth anxious night, when I woke suddenly after being unable, in the latest version of my dream, to find my shoes.

My first dream, in its summoning of the Buddhist phrase "unable to find what I was formerly sure was there," spoke to a specific discovery of the Buddha, one that emerged from his own curiosity and helped him resolve his own trauma. In the Buddhist approach, the ultimate target of mindfulness meditation is the sense of self. The active side of meditation takes it as a challenge to locate the self we intrinsically believe in and uses emotional experience as an opportunity to exercise this investigation. When one is upset or anxious or frustrated or angry, one tries to find "who" is feeling these things at the same time as one explores the feelings. The search is for what is sometimes called the "intrinsic identity habit" or the "intrinsic identity instinct," the way we unconsciously take ourselves to be "absolutely" real, as if we are really here, *absolutely*; fixed, enduring and all alone; intensely real and separate; in what is often called, in Buddhist psychology, "the cage of self-absolutization." Robert Thurman, a professor of religion at Columbia, quotes his old Mongolian Buddhist lama, whom he met in suburban New Jersey in the early 1960s, as explaining to him, "It's not that you're not real. We all think we're real, and that's not wrong. You are real. But you think you're *really* real, you exaggerate it." The picture we present to ourselves of who we think we ought to be obscures who we really are.

My first dream reminded me of this principle. Without my car, without the vehicle of my conveyance, without the self that needs to keep everything together, I began to come undone. But the stability offered by the meditation retreat, by mindfulness itself, made the dislodging of my ego's preeminence interesting. Over the course of the retreat, I got to explore myself in a richer and deeper way. The broken, interrupted, and fragmented dreams had room to express themselves.

And I, less attached to my need to be "really" real, could actually listen to them. What I discovered parallels the experience of the young woman in my workshop who heard her father's ringtone out of the blue. More connected to lost and broken aspects of myself, I felt myself opening up.

My friend Sharon Salzberg, a Buddhist teacher and cofounder of the retreat center I was at, tells a story about her own intensive meditation experience that is similar. In her case, it involved not anxiety but sorrow. Sharon was meditating under the auspices of a very accomplished and strict Burmese meditation master. She had to go to him many times a day and report what she was experiencing in her meditations, giving him a virtual moment-to-moment rendition of what was unfolding in her mind. These meetings had an air of formality about them. They did not last long, although they were frequent, and the master could be gruff, reserved, and intimidating. On this retreat, she was crying quite a bit while she was meditating, but she was uncomfortable telling him the extent of her sadness and somewhat ashamed of the intensity of her feelings. They did not seem to fit with her expectations of herself or with what the practice was supposed to bring any more than the angst of my dreams fit with mine.

Sharon's experience on her retreat presented her with a dilemma, one that was highlighted by the silence of the environment and her wish to have her teacher's approval. The self she was attached to, the person she thought she should be, and the image she had of herself did not encompass losing control of her emotions in this way. She resisted her feelings and downplayed them in her interviews.

When asked repeatedly what was happening in her meditations, she finally indicated that there was a *little* crying going on. "Are you crying a lot?" the Burmese master questioned her. "Not so much," she said, putting a brave face on. "When you cry in meditation," he responded, suddenly addressing her very personally, "you should cry with your whole heart."

The Burmese teacher's conversation with Sharon goes to the heart of the Buddha's understanding. The balance of mindfulness between relaxation and investigation allows us to enter into emotional experience in a full way while simultaneously offering us distance from it. This willingness to embrace disquiet, to "hold" it in meditative embrace, to give it life rather than abort it, is what turns out to be palliative. There is a secret agenda here, one that has its roots in the Buddha's own life history and one that the Burmese master undoubtedly was aware of when he gave Sharon his advice. The ego can easily trump its own goals. The effort that goes into protecting ourselves from uncomfortable feelings can have untoward consequences. Shutting down one kind of feeling inevitably shuts down all of them. In protecting ourselves from the unbearable affect of trauma, we also close ourselves off from love, joy, and empathy. Our humanity resides in our feelings, and we reclaim our humanity when we direct our curiosity at that which we would prefer to avoid. This was something the Buddha unexpectedly discovered for himself six years after replicating his own trauma and abandoning his wife and newborn child in what has become known as his "going forth."

When the Burmese master encouraged Sharon to cry with her whole heart, he was inviting her *into* her sadness, suggesting that she explore it with the curiosity that mindfulness fosters. In trying to keep it at bay, she was unknowingly giving it power over her, making it "really real" in the effort to diminish it and make it "really" unreal. Her teacher was trying to help her heal a split she had created: her ego on one side and her sorrow on the other. He understood that, in crying "with her whole heart," Sharon could recover not just her emotional pain but her emotional presence. This was his secret agenda: to undermine the ego's need to protect itself from painful affect and thereby restore its emotional foundation. Mindfulness dropped Sharon into the space between her ego and her unwanted emotion; it positioned her within the split she had made for herself and allowed her to look around. Her teacher, with the wisdom born of similar experience, gave her the key to rapprochement, the means to overcome her self-denigration, and the chance to be at one with herself. It wasn't just self-observation, and it wasn't only surrendering into the feeling. In asking her to bring those qualities together, to cry with her whole heart, the Burmese teacher was also showing her something she did not know about her mind. It could use her pain for its own development.

Going Forth

While the use of emotional experience to develop the mind became the keystone of the Buddha's psychology, this was not something he grasped right away. He had his own journey of discovery, one that has been memorialized in the stories of his enlightenment told over the centuries. His process was an interesting one. It began with a dramatic replication of the trauma he underwent when his mother passed away. This time, it was the Buddha who left abruptly. Just after the birth of his first child, he abandoned his wife and family to seek spiritual sustenance in the wilds of the Indian forests. His mind-set at the time of his "great departure" was radically different from where he ended up. It was much closer to Sharon's tendency to distance herself from her sorrow or to my own dissociation from my anxiety than to the Burmese master's understanding of the relationship of suffering to grace.

It took the Buddha a long time to figure things out. In his early life, as we have seen, he was clearly indulged. However we interpret the stories of his growing up—whether we imagine him protected behind the palace walls from any knowledge of death, illness, or old age, or whether we see him caged by conceit so that he could not relate to others who were suffering—it is clear that he was raised to not have to think about unpleasant things like the death of his mother. He was protected, as much as humanly possible, from the traumatic underpinnings of life. For a long time, he accepted this as the status quo and felt entitled to it. He liked his lily pools, his sandalwood, his Benares silks, and the white sunshade held over him. But at some point, the unreliable nature of material comforts began to reveal itself. Death, old age, and illness began to intrude, and the conceit he had grown up with began to seem objectionable. Gotama had a rather violent reaction. He left everything, in what has come to be called his "going forth," and set out to destroy his attachments.

A famous story in the Pali Canon about one of the Buddha's first followers, a rich merchant's son from Benares named Yasa, explores this very theme. Yasa's story, like that of the Four Messengers, has, over time, melded into the Buddha's own biography, so that many people think the events described happened to the Buddha rather than to him. But the Pali Canon is very clear about it. Soon after giving his first discourse on the Four Noble Truths and just before his famous Fire Sermon, in the first flush of his enlightenment, the Buddha had a pivotal exchange with Yasa. Their encounter was a spontaneous one, the first he was to have with someone from the merchant class, and similar to one a contemporary therapist might have with someone suffering from panic attacks or phobias. It grew out of a sudden crisis in Yasa's mind, an anxiety attack that eventually brought him face to face with the Buddha. Their exchange sheds enormous light on the revolution in the Buddha's own thinking. For Yasa was struggling with something the Buddha had also wrestled with—and resolved.

Yasa, like the Buddha, was raised in privilege and delicately brought up. Like the Buddha, his family also had three houses, one for the winter, one for the summer, and one for the rains. For the four months of the rainy season, he never went down to the city, staying in his country house where he was entertained nightly by female minstrels. He had quite the life. One evening, Yasa and his attendants fell asleep early. While it was dark outside, an all-night lamp burned dimly in their room. Before dawn, Yasa awoke and saw the women sleeping all around him in various states of disarray, their images partially distorted in the shadows created by the burning light. One woman was sleeping with her lute under her arm and another with her tambourine under her chin, while a third had her small drum nestled beneath her. "The hair of one had come unfastened, another was dribbling, others were muttering. It seemed like a charnel ground. When he saw it, when its squalor squarely struck him, he was sick at heart, and he exclaimed, 'It is fearful, it is horrible.'"[1]

Yasa went running out of his house, the dire images of the beloved female musicians disgusting him so. Not quite ready to abandon all vestiges of luxury, he paused as he was going out to put on his gold slippers and then proceeded to walk to the city's edge, to the deer park at Isipatana, where the Buddha was camping with his five ascetic followers, newly enlightened after hearing his first discourses. The Buddha had risen before dawn and was pacing back and forth in the park, getting his blood moving while doing his walking meditation. When he saw Yasa approaching in the distance, his golden slippers shining in the early-morning light, he sat down and waited for his arrival. As Yasa approached the Buddha, he called out, once again, "It is fearful, it is horrible!" Obsessive rumination had taken root in his mind.

Over the years, I have seen references to this story many times. It is depicted in countless works of art and described, with various embellishments, in many versions of the life of the Buddha. Most often, though, it is told as if it were Gotama waking in his palace and seeing his own allegedly desirable attendants in a ghastly light. The episode is commonly portrayed as the immediate instigation for his abandonment of his wife and child, the Buddha's first glimpse of the underside of carnal desire. I have always shied away from this tale because of its implicit condemnation of sensual desire and the way it disparages the women, making caricatures of them. I understand the ostensible teaching that lust disappoints, that beauty fades, and that addiction to sexual excitement becomes a misery, but I have a hard time, in many of the story's iterations, with the disgust the protagonist feels upon seeing the slobbering sleepers. It comes too close to the widespread male fear of female sexuality, or to male disparagement of sexuality in general, to make me comfortable. In many versions of the story, for example, the artists take great delight in rendering the attendants as prostitutes, painting them lasciviously while having the virtuous male protagonist stalk off. The judgment involved has always seemed to me unworthy of a Buddhist fable.

It was not until I actually started reading the sutras for myself that I discovered that the common renderings of this story are not the original ones. The level of subtlety in the sutras is much greater. The Buddha, upon hearing Yasa's panicked exclamations, did not support them. While he, too, during his phase of self-mortification, might once have responded similarly, he moved Yasa in a different direction. In an intimate conversation with the panic-stricken merchant's son, the Buddha began to articulate his own unique understanding of the importance of curiosity, even in the face of the worst.

"This is not fearful," explained the Buddha, "this is not horrible. Come, Yasa, sit down. I shall teach you the Dhamma."

Yasa was immediately relieved. "'This is not fearful, it seems, this is not horrible,'" he repeated, "and he was happy and hopeful. He took off his gold slippers and went to where the Blessed One was."[2] Then, according to the text, the Buddha laid out a sequence of teachings. He took Yasa through a condensed version of what would eventually come to be called Buddhism. At the core was an effort to reorient Yasa, to teach him an attitude toward the world that was not frightened or judgmental but was, instead, at once realistic and hopeful. The seeds of this attitude lay in the Buddha's own transformational journey, in which he moved from a similar tendency toward dissociation to a stance based in relaxation, investigation, and curiosity, in which he abandoned the extremes of self-indulgence and self-judgment (and self-torture) and embraced the joyful kindness essential to human nature. As the text describes it, Yasa sat down to the side of the Buddha.

"When he had done so, the Blessed One gave him progressive instruction, that is to say, talk on giving, on virtue, on the heavens; he explained the dangers, the vanity and the defilement in sensual pleasures and the blessings in renunciation. When he saw that Yasa's mind was ready, receptive, free from hindrance, eager and trustful, he expounded to him the teaching peculiar to the Buddhas: suffering, its origin, its cessation, and the path to its cessation. Just as a clean cloth with all marks removed would take dye evenly, so too while Yasa sat there the spotless, immaculate vision of the Dhamma arose in him: All that is subject to arising is subject to cessation."[3] This image of Yasa as a clean cloth taking the dye evenly is important. It suggests, in allegorical rather than psychodynamic language, that he was no longer dissociating aspects of himself. There was no longer a split between his ego and his unwanted feelings; there were no wrinkles or tangles to obstruct the fluidity of the Buddha's insights. And with this as a foundation, Yasa was able to tolerate the traumatic truth: All that arises is subject to cessation.

Yasa's first response, that his vision was fearful and horrible, speaks to the traumatic nature of his insight. He saw something that broke through one of his core "absolutisms of daily life" and made him sick at heart. Perhaps he had the sudden understanding that the sensual pleasures he was relying on to support his ego were inherently insubstantial. Or maybe he was confronted with the pain of his own addictive craving. A careful reading of the sutra suggests that Yasa's crisis was an existential one. It was as if he saw through the props he was using to avoid the traumatic underpinnings of life. His vision of his female attendants in disarray opened him briefly to the unstable nature of reality, but he could not sustain his insight. It frightened him and he cast about for someone or something to blame. Buddhist culture has unwittingly replicated his defensive maneuver. Why not blame the women? Or sexuality? Or both? In responding in this way, Yasa was actually mimicking the Buddha's own initial tendencies, and this is undoubtedly why their stories have become conflated. He was making the same mistake that the Buddha had made, one that had taken him six years to correct. For the Buddha, too, sought first to deal with the trauma of everyday life by taking extreme measures. He also felt that things were fearful and horrible and that he was "not safe," and he tried whatever he could find to make those feelings go away. But by the time Yasa came to him, he had established a different approach. He had found a way to make the experience of groundlessness nourishing rather than frightening.

On my most recent retreat at the Forest Refuge, a year after the one filled with anxious dreams, I had a moment that reminded me of Yasa. Perhaps it is too much of a stretch to make the comparison—it is not as though there were female musicians in states of disarray to frighten me in the middle of the night—but I did have an experience of the ground being pulled out from under me, and I could sense how unnerving it could be. It happened at breakfast toward the end of my week there. I had been craving toast for several days. The food had been remarkably good, but I had gotten it in my head that what was lacking was fresh-baked bread. It didn't seem like such a big thing to wish for—the vegetarian meals just needed this one little touch to feel complete. On this morning, six days into my stay, the bread finally appeared. Granted, it was gluten free and made from chickpea flour, but it still looked good. I cut myself a slice, toasted and buttered it, took a little bit of apricot jam, made myself a cup of tea, and settled silently into my seat to relish it all. I was very mindful and lifted the toast to my lips to take a bite. It was delicious. I chewed and tasted and swallowed and noticed how I wanted the next bite before I had completely finished the first. When the sweetness faded and the remnants of toast turned to cardboard in my mouth, I was ready for more. I waited, though, remembering the instructions for mindful eating: Finish each mouthful completely before taking the next bite.

I have only a vague recollection of what happened next. I believe my mind wandered to the laundry I had to do the next morning. There wasn't that much to think about anymore, but that didn't seem to be stopping me. Would I do one load or two? Could I put them both in at the same time? My wife would be happy if I came home with all my clothes washed. The next thing I remember was that my toast was gone. "Who ate my toast?" my mind cried as I stared at my empty plate. And for a brief second, before the humor of the situation could take hold, the whole thing became a metaphor for my entire life. Ready to relish it and it was already gone. I was staring into a big, empty, devouring hole where my toast, and my life, used to be. "Who ate my toast?" I repeated once again as I swiped my finger at the few crumbs left on the plate.

I had an immediate identification with Yasa. "It is fearful, it is horrible!" I understood where he was coming from. He had seen the dark side of his female attendants and I had witnessed the disappearance of my toast. The yawning jaws of death were all around me and I had a choice. I could panic or I could return to my mindfulness. I decided to go for a walk.

In the early 1980s, a Dutch psychologist named Johan Barendregt wrote a paper on the origin of phobias that is relevant to the Buddha's conversation with Yasa and to my lost breakfast moment. Barendregt proposed that phobias and related fears have their origins in intimations of groundlessness. Like Yasa glimpsing the traumatic underpinnings of life, or me staring into the place where my toast used to be, these perceptions of the impermanent and impersonal nature of things strip away the absolutisms of daily life that we rely upon. Such glimpses come unpredictably and in many guises. They may appear when people are smoking marijuana or traveling in a foreign country or listening to music or sitting in church. Most people cannot handle them and rush to replace them with something they *can* handle, even if it is an obsessive fear or anxiety. The beast we know is better than the one we do not. Barendregt quoted Rilke as wishing he had the "*courage de luxe*" to face up to "it," and he went on to describe, in the behaviorist language he was comfortable with, how his anxious patients attempted to describe what "it" was: "What 'it' means is described vaguely and indirectly, because the very essence of 'it' is bewilderment. 'It' is the experience that one's existing repertoire of categories of perception, thought and feeling—the systems and behavioral patterns that make it possible to organize one's perceptions and respond meaningfully—no longer suffice, and that one is no longer able to assign meanings, see connections or act functionally; 'it' is the experience of disorganization or—to put it in perhaps too extreme terms—irrationality."[4]

Barendregt's conclusion was that most obsessive anxieties and fears are reactions to the terrifying intimation of one's own insubstantiality. The *situation* in which the vision of chaos takes place becomes the focus of the fear rather than the vision itself. So someone like Yasa would become panicked at female sexuality because that was the setting in which his tenuous insight occurred. I might develop obsessive or compulsive rituals around food because my terror was aroused in the context of eating a piece of toast. We dissociate from that which seems unbearable and reorient ourselves around something we can conceive of. As Barendregt described his patients' predicament, "This 'it' situation is so unreal, so absurd, that they desperately try to recover their bearings and find them in fear, which is preferable to the void of 'it.' Since their fear is itself a very negative experience, coping mechanisms are developed to channel and rationalize it."[5]

When the Buddha sat down with Yasa, he helped him avoid this common pitfall. He countered Yasa's obsessive anxiety and gave him the means to integrate his vision of depersonalization. Much as Sharon had hoped to keep her Burmese teacher, and herself, from the depths of her sadness, Yasa was trying his best to keep the impact of his revelation at bay. Fleeing from his disturbing insight, he came to the Buddha with his bruised ego firmly in the lead. In his repetition of the phrase "It is fearful, it is horrible," we can see the telltale beginnings of a phobia. The Buddha, however, redirected Yasa, helping him to *see* impermanence, rather than supporting his fear of it. Notice that he did not tell Yasa that sensual pleasure *was* a defilement, as many Buddhists believe; he showed him *the defilement and the vanity* in sensual pleasure: the way people use sensual pleasure to avoid dealing with the truth of insubstantiality. There is an important difference here, one that is key to the Buddha's teachings. Pleasure is not the problem, the Buddha taught: Attachment is. While this insight is now enshrined in the practice of mindfulness, it was not an approach that came easily to the Buddha. He had a lot to work out in the process of discovering it.

In his first forays into homelessness, the Buddha turned away from the preoccupations of family life. Just as Yasa could not help blaming his terrifying vision on his female attendants, the Buddha at first thought householder life to be the problem. Like Yasa, he seems to have had a moment of existential dread when the reality of old age, illness, and death could not be avoided. After leaving his wife and newborn son, he went to the forest to study with the most accomplished therapists, the most adept meditators, of his day and age. There was already a strong and well-established tradition of yoga, meditation, and renunciation in the forests of northern India, and Gotama set out to learn from the acknowledged masters of his time and place, people who had already rejected everyday life, with its emphasis on material acquisitions and sensual pleasure, and held it in contempt. There were essentially two types of practice available to him, one that used yoga and meditation to reach for the sublime and the other that relied on self-punishment to achieve a state of invulnerability. One reached for the infinite sky of the transcendental spirit, while the other sought to tame the restless and boisterous sea of the body and the passions. These two strains of spiritual striving have a long history in South Asia. They predated the Buddha by thousands of years and have survived to this day, long after Buddhism virtually disappeared in India in the face of Islamic conquest a thousand years ago.

Gotama rather quickly mastered the transcendental practices— he found two highly realized masters but left each disappointed with the scope of their accomplishments. Despite learning to stabilize his mind and evoke prolonged mystical states of oneness or merger, he was unable to find lasting relief in these oceanic meditative states. In some way, he was mimicking his mother's flight to the heaven realm, leaving behind his earthly preoccupations for the exalted abode of the gods. These experiences reinforced his tendency toward dissociation by removing him even more completely from his body and everyday mind, but they removed him in a way that left his preoccupation with the traumatic underpinnings of life untouched. When he returned from the sublime states of meditation, he was still there, with the same profound sense of dis-ease that continued to torment him. Upon questioning his teachers, he found that they, too, had not been able to conquer their most fundamental fears. They could suspend themselves in states of hypnotic equipoise, but they did not emerge from those states any more enlightened than when they entered them. Each offered to have him stay and take over his role as guru, but Gotama was not so inclined. Like a well-analyzed patient of our own time who, while finally clear about the childhood origins of her neuroses, still loses her temper with her husband and children, Gotama became disillusioned with the traditional approaches available to him. He turned, in frustration, to the competing ideology of his time, that of self-punishment and self-mortification.

If a therapist were to comment on the Buddha's going forth, he would most likely frame the commentary around the contrast between the Buddha's self-described delicate nature and the violence of his leaving home and subsequent ascetic practices. Trying hard to be a good son, to satisfy the demands of his father and stepmother, the Buddha constructed a "caretaker" self that we might label as "false," created for the benefit and protection of his parents but lacking in authenticity and therefore "delicate." Winnicott wrote a case study in 1969 of just such a patient, who was dominated by a scream that could not be expressed. She, too, had dissociated her earliest feelings and was troubled by her broken dreams. "It is always true to say when reviewing one of this patient's sessions that if she could scream she would be well," wrote Winnicott. "The great non-event of every session is screaming."[6] The Burmese master who counseled Sharon was making much the same point. In encouraging her to cry her heart out, he was countering her inclination to make crying the "great non-event" of every meditation session. Like the Burmese teacher, Winnicott felt that if his patient could cry her heart out, her psyche would grow.

In a beautiful passage in Winnicott's case history, dated though it might now seem, he described the theory behind much of his clinical work. "If we take the situation in which she is a child playing while her mother is occupied with some activity such as sewing, this is the good pattern in which growth is taking place. At any moment the child may make a gesture and the mother will transfer her interest from her sewing to the child. If the mother is preoccupied and does not at first notice the child's need, the child has only to begin to cry and the mother is available. In the bad pattern which is at the root of this patient's illness, the child cried and the mother did not appear. In other words the scream that she is looking for is *the last scream just before hope was abandoned.* Since then screaming has been of no use because it fails in its purpose."[7]

Winnicott revealed something important about therapy in his case study. The best the therapist can do with a patient like this, he remarked, is to "give understanding." Like the Buddha with Yasa, he did not take the position that the situation was fearful and horrible but instead made room for a feeling that had been, over the years, dissociated. A compassionate attitude toward the bad pattern "points toward" the good pattern that had been long forgotten. "Profound understanding leads of course towards screaming, that is to say towards screaming again, this time with hope."[8]

Winnicott went on to describe how, some time into her therapy, his patient dreamed herself screaming and then began to notice significant relief in waking life. Much as I began to dream on my retreat, Winnicott's patient, safely ensconced in her relationship with him, found that she was also able to remember, and make use of, her dreams. Coincidentally to this process, she reported being able to sing at a community event. Dreaming of screaming led to her singing. And Winnicott described how she was then able to speak up when he was late to a session. Her anger was no longer felt to be impotent but could be martialed in service of the therapeutic relationship. "We need to dream our scream for it to become real and we need to experience our dream as part of the real-izing process,"[9] wrote Michael Eigen years later about this case.

Winnicott's case study illuminates something critical about the

Buddha's path. While he was not yet ready to dream his traumatized self, the Buddha, without realizing it at first, acted out his trauma in the pursuit of self-punishment and self-mortification. Like Yasa running from his disturbing vision of sexuality the Buddha became consumed with how fearsome and horrible human needs could be. Winnicott's case study describes how therapists now understand the evolution of this kind of shame. The raw vision of one's helplessness and dependency, the feeling of groundlessness, as exemplified in his case study by the mother who was not there to hear her child's scream, is too overwhelming to bear, too primordial to symbolize. It cannot be held by the mind. Something has to take its place, and this often takes the shape of a neurotic symptom or set of symptoms, a fear or a phobia or an obsessive determination to control one's body or mind. A conviction that there is something fundamentally wrong with oneself or one's world, painful though that might be, is more tolerable than staring into the void.

The bulk of Gotama's six years of wandering were spent in the company of five companions practicing austerities, the same five to whom he later gave the teachings of the Four Noble Truths and who then watched as he settled Yasa down and gave him hope. The general idea of their asceticism was that since pleasure led to attachment, the elimination of pleasure could break the hold of this illusory world and release one into the realm of pure spirit. By depriving the body of its everyday needs one could build up a kind of spiritual power or "heat" that could bring one into contact with the divine. If indulging one's needs for comfort, food, safety, or sex led to bondage, then a refusal to yield to one's desires must lead to freedom. Ascetic practitioners were widespread in the wilds of India in the Buddha's time—they can still be found, as Allen Ginsberg discovered on his first trip to India, on the periphery of Indian society today.

One of the most interesting things about reading traditional accounts of the Buddha's austerities is how aggressive he sounds. He is far from the delicate creature he once was. No longer clad in the expensive silks of Benares, he becomes as fierce as any matted-haired, fire-worshipping, snake-garlanded ascetic of his time. As the Buddha implied when he reflected upon his own delicate nature, he was raised in such a way that the most troubling feelings were kept apart from everyday life. As legend came to describe, walls were built around any intimation of death, destruction, or loss. In his ascetic practices, the Buddha turned all this around. If he had been shielded from distress in his childhood, he flung himself into it in the forest. One can almost hear a therapist like Winnicott describing the Buddha's "ruthless rejection of his own female element," with his "unwelcome male element threatening to take over his whole personality."[10]

Ascetic practices brought Gotama's aggression out into the open and gave it a means of expression. In making his own body/mind the object of assault, he found a safe object to attack, albeit one that was under constant threat of collapse. Gotama's spiritual pursuits had him hitting his head against the wall of his own suffering, trying to find relief through the attempted destruction of his own support. His ideal during this time, as recounted in the Pali Canon, was to become like a "dry, sapless piece of wood lying on dry land," ready, at the first opportunity, to burst into flames. The imagery is almost too perfect. Draining himself of all of what is called *rasa* in Sanskrit—the juice, flavor, taste, essence, or emotion of desire[11]—the Buddha was hoping to become free of his human foibles. He was literally attempting to empty himself of the sap that ran through his veins, turning himself into kindling for one of the sacrificial fires so common to the wandering forest ascetics.

By subjugating his passions, keeping himself walled off from temptation, and deliberately challenging his body, Gotama hoped that he could drain himself of instinct and leapfrog into the divine. With the juice squeezed out, Gotama expected to make himself a pure vehicle, one free of earthly toxins and capable of spiritual sublimation. He was aiming to go directly from solid to spirit through his own personal alchemy of self-deprivation. He was said to make four times the effort of the other recluses, such that he came to be called *Mahashramana*, the "Great Wanderer."[12] The traditional texts of the Pali Canon are unsparing in their descriptions of his dedicated self-abuse.

> I thought: "Suppose, with my teeth clenched and my tongue pressed against the roof of my mouth, I beat down, constrain and crush my mind with my mind?" Then, as a strong man might seize a weaker by the head or shoulders and beat him down, constrain him and crush him, so with my teeth clenched and my tongue pressed against the roof of my mouth, I beat down, constrained and crushed my mind with my mind. Sweat ran from my armpits while I did so.
>
> I thought: "Suppose I practise the meditation that is without breathing?" I stopped the in-breaths and out-breaths in my mouth and nose. When I did so, there was a loud sound of winds coming from my ear holes, as there is a loud sound when a smith's bellows are blown.
>
> I stopped the in-breaths and out-breaths in my mouth and nose and ears. When I did so, violent winds racked my head, as if a strong man were splitting my head open with a sharp sword. And then there were violent pains in my head, as if a strong man were tightening a tough leather strap round my head, as a head-band. And then violent winds carved up my belly, as a clever butcher or his apprentice carves up an ox's belly with a sharp knife. And then there was a violent burning in my belly, as if two strong men had seized a

weaker man by both arms and were roasting him over a pit of
live coals.[13]

The Buddha goes on to describe how emaciated he became. Eating only a handful of food per day, his eyes sunk down in their sockets
as if at the bottom of a deep well; his scalp shriveled and withered like
a pumpkin left out in the wind and sun; his arms and legs like hollow bamboo stems; his ribs jutting out "like the crazy rafters of an
old roofless barn"; his vertebrae resembling corded beads poking
through his backside; his hair, rotted at its roots, dropping out in
clumps when he rubbed his head; and his body falling over on itself
when he urinated or moved his bowels; he was a wreck. His five fellow
penitents were rapt in his presence—never before had anyone taken
self-mortification to such an extreme. Gotama almost succeeded in
squeezing himself dry. He likened himself to a stone breaking a raw
clay pot or to a raw clay pot broken by a stone. Breaker and broken were
almost one. His five friends' exhilarated responses notwithstanding,
his intrinsic capacity to elicit a thrill of bliss in another was almost
extinguished.

At this point in the Buddha's story something incredible happened. Nothing supernatural, just a momentary thought. As Winnicott once wrote, describing how he had mellowed as a therapist in his
later years, "If only we can wait, the patient arrives at understanding
creatively and with immense joy."[14] A version of this happened for the
Buddha. Unbidden, a childhood memory came bubbling to the surface
of Gotama's mind. Out of the blue, as if from nowhere, a lost moment
arose. Stumbling over himself as he urinated, he was transported
back to his youth. Barely able to stand on his own two feet after years
of self-torture, the Buddha remembered himself as a boy, happily
sitting under a rose-apple tree, the sun shining, a warm breeze blowing, his father some distance away working in the fields, and his own

mind at peace. In some accounts he also remembered noticing insects, eggs, and worms cut up by the plow. He was overtaken, these accounts assert, by a "strange sorrow, as though it were his own relatives that had been killed,"[15] and compassion for the hapless creatures arose in his heart. In all the accounts of this memory, young Gotama was soon filled with tenderness and settled into the beautiful day, "and a feeling of pure joy rose up unbidden in his heart."[16] Sitting under the *jambu*, or rose-apple, tree, he was suffused with this feeling, as if he himself were the tree with the sap rising within. It is also said in some later versions that the shadow of the rose-apple tree did not move as the afternoon progressed. The shadow remained still, sheltering the young boy as he sat cross-legged beneath it,[17] marking the moment as a special one.

However peculiar to be suddenly overtaken by this memory at the height of self-mortification, even stranger was the fact that it made him anxious and afraid. "What is this fear about?" the Buddha wondered to himself, summoning the curiosity that was to become a hallmark of his method. "Maybe I should take a look."

In the self-analysis that followed, the Buddha came to the conclusion that the joy that had arisen under the rose-apple tree could well be something unexpectedly essential to the enlightenment he was seeking. Up until the dawning of this memory, he was driven by the belief that he had to purify himself of all feeling and lift himself out of his human embodiment to connect with something greater than himself. The defense of dissociation was, up to this point, unconsciously guiding his approach. In my analysis, he was also driven by his mother's inability to tolerate the bliss he brought her, an inability he must have internalized and used against himself, fueling his unworthiness. After investigating the memory, which was in some way a rediscovery of that very bliss, the Buddha changed his mind.

"'Why am I afraid of such pleasure? It is a pleasure that has nothing to do with sensual desires and unwholesome things.' Then I thought: 'I am not afraid of such pleasure,'" the Buddha considered, "'for it has nothing to do with sensual desires and unwholesome things.'"[18]

This was the Buddha's critical insight and the pivot point for his entire journey. It was the moment when he began to trust himself, when he stopped being seduced by the appearance of holiness and made himself, in his own words, "a lamp unto himself." His memory is talked about as the foundation of his Middle Path, the route he found between sensory indulgence on the one hand and self-loathing on the other. It was a new discovery, one that Winnicott was intuitively following in his clinical work, where he was fostering the conditions for self-knowledge by "giving understanding" to that which could not be ordinarily conceived. It was the moment when the Buddha began to chart a novel course for himself, going against the grain of his culture while opening up a new formula for self-investigation. And it was the moment when the defense of dissociation cracked and he arrived at his understanding, in Winnicott's words, "creatively and with immense joy."

The implications of the Buddha's discovery are relevant even in our time. There are certainly people, even today, who are torturing themselves with self-hatred or self-denial in an attempt to shake themselves free. Anorectic patients, for instance, refuse food with as mighty an intensity as the Buddha mustered, and it is often the case that they are refusing feelings as well, substituting an obsessive need for control for their more volatile emotional lives. There are less obvious variations on this theme. A recent patient of mine, a speechwriter in his late forties with a longstanding but private interest in Eastern spirituality, came to me for guidance in learning about Buddhism. He was surprised when I urged him to relax into his conscious awareness of whatever arose in his mind or body. "I thought the point was to get rid of that awareness," he said. Like the Buddha before his childhood memory, he wanted an escape from himself, imagining that the release of meditation was akin to a good rest. He was disoriented at first when he found that meditation, more than anything, made him more alert to the natural world. Walking in the forest with his young daughter, he was touched by how alive everything began to seem. The rest he was seeking came as a heightening of awareness, not a diminishment of it.

The Buddha's rejection of the extremes speaks to another tendency in our culture. In our flight from the traumatic underpinnings of everyday life, we have become the opposite of the abstemious Buddha. As I was prone to do with my toast on my retreat, we look to the accumulation of sensory pleasures to give our lives meaning. We have the ability now to consume anything we want, and this capacity far exceeds our actual needs. With so much at our fingertips, a kind of gluttony pervades our mind-sets. We are attached not only to our possessions and our passions but to our smart phones, our tablets, and our devices, obsessively consuming connection while, in the words of MIT professor Sherry Turkle, "avoiding conversation." This is another manifestation of the rush to normal that the Buddha warned against. We want to be like everybody else. We don't want to have to feel disease. We are wary even of the more subtle joys that arise unbidden when we get out of the way of ourselves. As Professor Turkle wrote recently in the *New York Times*, we want to be digitally in touch but often do so at the expense of a deeper conversation with one another and with ourselves. "I spend the summers at a cottage on Cape Cod," she wrote, "and for decades I walked the same dunes that Thoreau once walked. Not too long ago, people walked with their heads up, looking at the water, the sky, the sand and at one another, talking. Now they often walk with their heads down, typing. Even when they are with friends, partners, children, everyone is on their own devices. So I say, look up, look at one another, and let's start the conversation."[19]

The Buddha would have agreed with Sherry Turkle. In the moment of his childhood memory he looked up from his smart phone and unhooked himself from his obsessive self-preoccupation. He, too, was trying to be like everybody else, or at least like the very best holy man he could imagine. But, lucky for him, he had a spontaneous experience that surprised him. He felt the fear that often provokes a phobic response, but his curiosity protected him. He looked at his fear and it did not make sense. He began a conversation with himself that continued for the next several weeks and that culminated in his enlightenment. And he continued that conversation for many more years, with Yasa as one of his first contacts.

While the Buddha erred on the side of self-denial, not self-indulgence, his core understanding pertained to both. Up until his childhood memory, the Buddha had not recognized that the seeds of liberation were already present within. The spontaneous arising of his memory provoked a recalibration of his psyche. It resolved his conflict over how to relate to himself. If the joy he remembered under the rose-apple tree was not a result of the blind pursuit of pleasure, if it had nothing to do with sensual desires, then it must be intrinsic to the Buddha's own nature. If it was intrinsic to his nature, then there was no need to turn himself into a stone or a dry, sapless piece of wood, no need to erode the physical and mental substrate of his being. If this joy was a key to enlightenment, then his approach had to change. How could he use this remembered joy to guide him on his path? He could investigate it rather than trying to wipe it out: He could engage it in conversation.

The first thing the Buddha decided was that if he wanted to sustain his joy, he needed to eat. "It is not possible to attain that pleasure with a body so excessively emaciated. Suppose I ate some solid food— some boiled rice and bread?"[20] At this point in the story, a maiden appeared, a young village woman named Sujātā, who brought him some porridge or rice pudding called *kummāsa*. The five ascetics who had been cheering him on grew disgusted when they saw him with her. They thought he had gone soft, lost his edge, become a convert to some other guru, the way we might feel when a respected professor suddenly discovers the New Age. "The monk Gotama has become self-indulgent, he has given up the struggle and reverted to luxury,"[21] they cried. They left him and wandered on, searching for new inspiration. In the legends that have grown up in Buddhist culture over the years, this incident has taken on special meaning. As if to drive home the relationship between the Buddha's childhood memory and the return of his lost mother, Sujātā is described in one famous text as having been the Buddha's mother in five hundred previous existences.[22] In another text she is remembered as a village girl who prayed to a local tree deity that she might give birth to a son. When her wish comes true, she brings an offering to the tree, sees the Buddha there, and assumes he is the tree god incarnate. In this version, the Buddha is recognized as having transformed from a dry piece of kindling into the essence of the tree itself. A psychoanalytic reading of the story would, of course, focus on the image of the breast. Sujātā's feeding of *kummāsa* to the Buddha, in support of his childhood joy, evokes the short-lived mother-child union that drove his mother into retreat.

The Buddha, in the aftermath of his meal, did not swing back to an embrace of luxury. He actually resolved something. There was a middle way, he decided. While he did not have to be driven by his feelings, by his body, or by his thoughts, he did not have to eliminate them either. His understanding deepened and his tolerance for ambiguity soared. His whole approach to meditation took a radical turn. Instead of seeking to break his mind with his mind, he let the joy of his childhood memory and the curiosity it evoked infuse and inform his technique. He let it become the platform for his awakening. While not forsaking the self-inquiry he had already begun, he let up on himself.

He noted that his pleasure-driven thoughts and feelings, if carefully observed, did not provoke him to act. Like bubbles in a stream, they would come to the surface of his mind and pop. By not identifying with them, by not being caught up in their content, he could have access to a deeper joy, one that bore a stark resemblance to that which he had stumbled upon, and then forgotten about, in his childhood under the rose-apple tree and one that went all the way back to the thrill of bliss he had evoked in his mother at birth. Later, after his enlightenment, he called this new way of relating "mindfulness."

The Buddha's discovery empowered him. In a short time, after walking to the site of the present-day Indian village Bodh Gaya and sitting under a large fig tree by the banks of the Neranjara River, he was filled with a rush of realizations. Primary among them was a fundamental shift in the way he approached himself. As one of his biographers, Karen Armstrong, has described it, he no longer had to pounce on his failings but could use his reflective awareness to become acquainted with how his mind worked, in order to "exploit its capacities."[23] His days of dissociation were over. In its place was a newfound ability, one very similar to that discovered by Winnicott when he broke himself of his need to show off his intelligence to his patients and learned to wait for the joy of their self-discoveries. "I now enjoy this joy more than I used to enjoy the sense of having been clever,"[24] wrote Winnicott. The Buddha found something similar. In enjoying his joy, he allowed his mind to unfurl. In a carefree gesture long celebrated in Buddhist traditions, upon finishing his milk rice the Buddha tossed his bowl into the river. It floated upstream, signifying the change in direction the Buddha now embraced, and then sank to the bottom of the river, nestling on top of the bowls of the three previous Buddhas from different eras, all of whom had had similar awakenings at the same spot. The clinking of one bowl striking the others was said to awaken the *naga*, or serpent, king dwelling there, alerting him to the proximity of yet another Buddha. This waking of the unconscious, as personified by the rousing of the serpent at the bottom of the river, was another way of describing the return of the Buddha's dissociated affect. No longer plagued by a feeling of not fitting in, and no longer tortured by the belief in his own intrinsic badness, the Buddha-to-be embraced the thrill of bliss that had driven his mother to distraction. With this joy as his support and his humanity restored, his journey to enlightenment gathered momentum.

8

Feelings Matter

The Buddha once gave a teaching in response to his followers'
repeated requests to explain the mysteries of the universe to
them. Known to possess a "divine eye," the Buddha was asked
over and over again to talk about how everything really worked. Okay,
he finally cried. I give up. You want to know about the world? I'll tell
you. The world that matters is what you experience. The world is your
eyes, ears, nose, mouth, body, and mind; your sights, sounds, smells,
tastes, sensations, thoughts, and feelings; the visual, aural, olfactory,
gustatory, kinesthetic, and intuitive consciousnesses that accompany
them. Like a contemporary neurobiologist, the Buddha explained how
each of his disciples was constantly remaking the world through his
own sense organs, breaking it down and reconstructing it through
his own relational mental processes. You and the world are not really
separate, he explained, although that's the way it seems. In fact, each
person, each organism, is inextricably interwoven into the fabric of the
world, constantly reproducing a version of it through their interactive, sense-based, experience of it. The self is not the same as any of
these processes, nor could it be said to exist separately from them, he
affirmed. The self is a mystery. In our efforts to pin it down or make it

safe, we dissociate ourselves from our complete experience of whatever it is or is not. While other spiritual disciplines counseled a rejection of the body, suppression of the emotions, or the eradication of the personality in the hopes of connecting with a divine soul or spirit or essence that could survive death, the Buddha taught his students simply to attend to the shifting landscape of mind and body. Nothing else matters, he claimed. Only this.

This way of speaking was the Buddha's introduction to his biggest discovery, known in its shorthand version as the doctrine of "no-self." The shorthand version is a bit of a problem, because the Buddha's teachings on the subject were actually quite nuanced and always varied depending on whom he was talking to. If the person believed strongly in a concrete soul or self or spirit, the Buddha would emphasize its empty nature, but if they believed in an empty self, if they were convinced they were vacant or hollow or unworthy or didn't matter, he would tell them that too was mistaken, that they were attached to emptiness, that their human birth was immensely precious. For the supersophisticated, he would often say there is neither self nor nonself and then further confuse them by saying that if they took that too seriously they would be wrong too. His efforts were always in the service of releasing people from their fixed ideas about who or what they were, about freeing them from attachment to whatever concept they were clinging to, about loosening the hold that the fear-based ego claimed as its birthright. The Buddha understood the traumas of everyday life, but he was determined to challenge both the protective reactions of dissociation and the underlying hopelessness that accompanies them.

To this end—as he did for all of the individuals, like Yasa and Paṭācārā, who came to him in distress—he taught the Four Foundations of Mindfulness. Preserved in the Pali Canon in a sutra called the *Satipaṭṭhāna Sutta*, his instructions were remarkably clear and straightforward. They codified his pivotal understanding that the path out of fear and dissociation depends on the ability to use reflective awareness to study the nature of everyday experience. For the Buddha, this was not some kind of elevated philosophical inquiry. It meant the actual investigation, in real time, of the moment-to-moment unfolding of the mental, emotional, and physical components of the self. That is why, in his lecture to his followers on the mysteries of the universe, he stressed the centrality of the five senses and the mind. He made much the same argument in his sutra on mindfulness.

The Four Foundations of Mindfulness are the domains of personal experience—the foci—in which mindfulness can be practiced. The Buddha specified them as consisting of the body (or breath), feelings, the mind, and mental objects like thoughts and emotions. This was another way of breaking down subjective experience so that it could be opened up to meditative scrutiny, just as he did in his teaching on the nature of the universe. After rejecting his ascetic attempts to suppress his physical and emotional self, the Buddha came to see that freedom actually came from within. The sutra on the Four Foundations of Mindfulness was his way of describing how to make that freedom happen.

The Buddha structured his teachings on the foundations of mindfulness in a very careful way. Recognizing, from his own obsessive immersion in austerity, that the most common reaction to the trauma of everyday life was a flight from bodily experience, he made mindfulness of the body the first foundation of his teaching. This was his way of countering the grossest form of dissociation, known in today's psychological language as "derealization," in which the defense of dissociation is applied to physical experience. In severe trauma, after rape or war or abuse or horrible accidents, this kind of reaction is well-known. Nothing seems real. The body seems alien. Physical things lose their solidity. But there is a spectrum of this kind of dissociation, as therapists have come to realize. The character armor that hardens muscles while protecting people from being emotionally hurt also limits their availability: to life, to love, to themselves and others. Children who suffer from developmental trauma, as Winnicott always pointed out, flee from their physical experience to a haven in their minds he called their "caretaker self" and suffer from a reduced sense of their own vitality. The Buddha acted out this flight from the body in his six years of austerities, and he enshrined its reversal in his first foundation. By using the body as a beginning focus of meditation, by gradually easing oneself into the moment-to-moment reality of physical embodiment, the mind begins to learn an alternative to dissociation.

The first foundation of mindfulness is very specific. It involves watching the breath enter and leave the body or, in some of the many variations that have been developed over time, listening to sounds come and go or watching physical sensations arise and pass away. It focuses on what are called the five sense doors—the eyes, ears, mouth, nose, and body—and guides the attention to the bare facts of what each sense organ registers at the boundary between the internal and the external environments. It can be applied to physical activities like walking or eating and is the mainstay of what has come to be known as "sitting" meditation practice. But this is only the beginning: the first of the four foci the Buddha knew to be important for training the mind. The second foundation, mindfulness of feelings, is the bridge between the body and the mind. It is the one that the Buddha's childhood memory alerted him to, the one that took him out of his attachment to asceticism and returned him to the world.

According to the Buddha's psychology, feelings are always present. They accompany every moment of awareness. They can be pleasant, unpleasant, or neutral, and they can be based in the body or in the mind. They flow continuously, although we tend to intervene reactively, dissociating from the painful feelings, clinging to the pleasant ones, and ignoring the neutral. Our egos, in our relentless rush to normal, pull us away from our feelings when they are difficult and immerse us in them unconditionally when they are alluring. In the practice of mindfulness, these habitual tendencies in relationship to our feelings are countered. One learns to abide in the flow of feeling, not pushing away the uncomfortable and not hanging on to the pleasurable. A deepening of internal experience inevitably results.

The Buddha came to accept the importance of feelings when he recovered his childhood memory and saw that he was afraid of the pleasure it held. In that tiny but crucial moment the Buddha saw the importance of both unpleasant and pleasant feeling, of both fear and joy. His interest in his own emotional experience was piqued and he began a new process of attending, without judgment, to both the pleasant and unpleasant aspects of mental and emotional life. Opening himself to his own subjective flow of feeling, he stopped trying to make it go away. He realized that he mattered, that he did not have to destroy himself, even as he was setting the stage for an equally profound realization: that he was not the limited individual he thought he was.

At that moment, remembering his childhood joy, he also made the crucial distinction between "sensual" and "nonsensual" feelings that became an essential part of his teachings on mindfulness. Sensual feelings were clearly dependent on sensory events, and their pleasant, unpleasant, or neutral qualities were easy to apprehend. But "nonsensual," or "nonworldly" feelings, like the kind he recovered in his childhood memory, were more mysterious. They seemed to be experienced in the mind as much as in the body, and they carried hints of the past while also being able to fill the mind in the present. This distinction between the two kinds of feelings freed him up and gave him a new approach to working with the anguish, or *dukkha*, that had driven him into the forest in the first place. It showed him another kind of pleasure besides the physical one that was less dependent on sensory gratification and more related to simple being. And it gave shape and history to the fear that had propelled his spiritual search in the first place. He was able to make this fear an object of inquiry instead of something he needed to run away from. In reorienting himself in this way, the Buddha was firmly in line with the psychotherapy tradition of our own time. Accepting the importance of internal feelings, the Buddha opened himself to the mystery of the self. He validated psychological experience and made the psyche, as he had the body, available for subjective exploration.

As the great contemporary scholar of Buddhism at Oxford, Richard Gombrich, has repeatedly pointed out, people tend to construe the Buddhist concept of no-self or no-soul as "denying a principle of continuity."[1] Gombrich pulls no punches when addressing this misconception. "That is totally wrong," he asserts. "The idea that Buddhism denies personal continuity could not be further from the truth."[2] The Buddha taught that there is no unchanging essence in people or in things, that what we ordinarily take to be objects are, in fact, processes, but he did not deny the sense of individual subjectivity, of interiority, or of personal continuity. In fact, the general thrust of his teachings was to encourage exactly that sense of personal continuity that people mistakenly think he denied, a continuity that derives in good part from the flow of feeling that underlies our lives.

In the Buddha's uncovering of the Middle Path lay a profound and fundamental shift in the spiritual approach to pleasure and unpleasure. The dominant spiritual ideology of his time suggested that pleasant feelings were to be shunned[3] and unpleasant feelings cultivated for their purifying effects. The Buddha, who tried his best to emulate this approach, was ultimately urged into a confrontation with this ideology and turned it on its head. He did not swing to the opposite, to the materialist stance that was widespread in his time and remains dominant in ours, where we believe that unpleasant feelings should be avoided and pleasant ones accumulated for their invigorating effects, but he opened up the realm of feelings, in all of their variety, to meditative scrutiny. This led him directly to the third and fourth foundations of mindfulness, to the potential of mind and mental objects as vehicles of meditative examination. Nothing in the psyche needs to be excluded, the Buddha taught. It can all be held in a meditative embrace. In today's psychodynamic language, we might say that the Buddha discovered the unconscious and put it to use as grist for the spiritual mill.

The Buddha did not call it the unconscious, however; he simply called it "mind." The mind has its own capacity for feeling, he deduced, over and above the corporeal dimension of the five traditional senses. His embrace of the mental dimension of pleasure and pain, which involved opening himself to the interior of his psyche—to its memories, dreams, and reflections and to its continuity over time—allowed him to expand the scope of meditation. No longer idealizing the peaceful quiescence of hypnotic tranquility and no longer trying to escape from himself, the Buddha saw that it was possible to "give understanding" not only to the pleasant and painful aspects of mental feeling but to the entirety of personal experience. The mind itself could become an object of mindfulness.

Just as the Buddha used mindfulness of the body, the first foundation, as a platform for exploring feelings, he used mindfulness of feelings, the second foundation, as a way into the mind. There are various ways of interpreting and describing the third and fourth foundations of mindfulness, the examination of mind and mental objects, but the direction of the Buddha's approach is clear. As the tendency toward dissociation is countered, first by examination of physical experience and then by an acceptance of the flow of feelings, mental and emotional life becomes more available. Much of the sutra on the fourth foundation of mindfulness, for instance, deals with how to skillfully pay attention to anger, greed, doubt, agitation, and withdrawal, the emotional "hindrances" to mindfulness that come flooding out of the psyche—out of the unconscious—when the first efforts toward mindful awareness are made. Their appearance, while the cause of much frustration, fear, and shame, is actually a positive sign. They are often among the first indications of the opening of the internal landscape. They stop being obstacles when we learn to "hold" them in meditative awareness.

The most esoteric aspect of the Four Foundations of Mindfulness has to do with what is called mindfulness of mind. It does not really mean observation of individual thoughts or emotions—this is covered in the fourth foundation under the rubric of mindfulness of mental objects. It has more to do with the ability of the mind to know itself knowing, if that makes any sense. In the beginning steps of this foundation, one learns simply to know, for example, what a mind filled with fear or a mind immersed in joy feels like. One is directed not so much toward the pleasantness or unpleasantness of the feeling, or even toward the texture of the emotion, as toward the shape or sensation or experience of the mind colored by a particular feeling. When the emotions are strong, it is not hard to shift perspective and feel how intensely they color the mind, especially if one is sitting in meditation all day deliberately doing nothing. But as the emotions calm down, it is still possible to observe the mind with the mind. The mind that knows knows itself knowing. It is quite strange, but at the same time it feels entirely natural. In some Tibetan Buddhist traditions, to make it more accessible, this is called mindfulness of space instead of mindfulness of mind. It is compared to the blue sky that appears when the clouds of grief and fear and vanity are burned off by the sun of mindful awareness. Empty, luminous, and knowing, it is said, the mind knows itself as it really is.

I can give a personal example of how this works. When I went to take my walk after my breakfast of the missing toast, I was still aware of a lurking dissatisfaction. I was ashamed, I realized, of my failure to be mindful in the morning. My feeling reminded me of how a visiting gallery dealer must have felt when he backed up and squatted down to take a photo of one of my wife's sculptures and sat on a fragile piece of porcelain he had not noticed and shattered it. The sound of the broken porcelain resounded through the gallery and he looked as if he might faint. I saw him berate himself and I could immediately relate to how he was feeling. "I can't believe I did that!" he must have scolded himself.

On my walk after breakfast I had the definite sensation of the trauma of the morning having not completely disappeared. My meditation did not seem to be releasing me the way I thought it should. My mind was more concentrated, as the Buddha wished it to be, but my thoughts were still there, as I did not. I often think that I shouldn't be thinking when on retreat but thinking is what my mind does, so I have to find a way to not turn it into a problem. As a result, I find myself watching my mind thinking about thinking, or thinking about not thinking, and I try not to think I am just wasting my time. The teachings on the Four Foundations of Mindfulness have helped me make room for this in my meditation.

That morning, my thoughts were particularly pronounced. I was walking. Not the ultra-slow, lifting/moving/placing, mindful walking I had been taught to do between sitting meditation periods, but a more normal stroll. I was taking a walk after breakfast on an old country road that looped around the outskirts of the retreat center. It was a ramshackle road but not without charm; full of trees, and woodland birds that skittered alongside as I walked, making me feel like Snow White or one of her seven dwarfs.

A couple of things were in my mind as I walked. The morning's lapse of mindfulness. My feelings of shame. The sense of my life disappearing out from under me. And the Buddha's teachings of no-self. It's hard to be on a Buddhist retreat without thinking about no-self. Every lecture insists on it. What is the self, we are constantly asked to consider. And Buddhist sutras, like the famous Diamond Sutra, are always ready with a metaphor or two. The self is but "a star at dawn, a bubble in a stream, a flash of lightning in a summer cloud, a flickering lamp, a phantom, and a dream," they suggest.

"Those are a lot of things for a no-self to be," I thought to myself as I strode along, eyeing the breaking of the late-autumn day, my self-preoccupation tugging at my mind. Did I understand it? I wasn't so sure. No-self must mean inner peace, the place beyond thought, the reservoir of contentment I sometimes found when I successfully let go of my usual preoccupations. But I had the uneasy sense that this was probably wrong. There was a famous story of a very learned and accomplished Tibetan master who, when he was finally enlightened, said, emphatically, that it was exactly the opposite of what he had imagined. I knew I was not enlightened. Therefore, by the logic of the Tibetan master, whatever I imagined no-self to be was probably one hundred and eighty degrees off. If no-self wasn't inner peace then what was it? I tried to feel like a bubble in a stream or a flickering light or a dream but I've never been much good at visualizing and I gave up before too long. I felt more like Snow White than a phantom or a bubble and my recurrent efforts to remember the names of her seven dwarfs kept interrupting my philosophical ruminations.

I couldn't do much with the concept of no-self that morning. "Can't figure it out right now," I thought to myself with a sigh. I realized I was trying to avoid the feelings hanging around from earlier in the morning. At that moment, I was suddenly aware of how much information my senses were sensing, my ears and eyes especially. The landscape surrounding me, filled with color and early morning light, and the rustling of the birds in the trees and undergrowth, were filling my consciousness. I had a brief flash of a diagram I had studied in medical school. Dotted lines connecting two inverted triangles—the eyes taking the world into the brain. I remembered how I used to think the eye was like a camera, faithfully reflecting the outside world in the theater of the mind. But then I had learned otherwise. It was vastly more mysterious than that. The brain actually creates our reality, I was taught, it does not just mirror it. Sensory data enter the brain as raw material, not as finished images. The eye perceives angles and edges, not objects or backgrounds. It's up to the brain to make reality coherent, building it up out of the raw information our organs of sight, smell, touch, taste, hearing and memory feed it.

Immersed in the sights and sounds surrounding me, this bit of basic science took on a more profound meaning as I meandered on my way. It wasn't as much "me" walking through "it" as it usually was. The dotted lines of the diagram began to seem as important as the triangles. "In here" and "out there," the two triangles I could see in my mind's eye, were not two different things: they were connected. This world I was walking through, stirring slightly in the faint morning air, was my mind. And my mind, its thoughts notwithstanding, was this world. Another phrase crossed my mind: one I had read somewhere recently in a Buddhist text but not really understood, "There is no self apart from the world." Now that phrase was resonating. Or resounding. No self apart from the world. I thought I understood what it meant. In here and out there. Not two. One.

It was a joyous experience to walk with that phrase percolating through me. It turned something around in my understanding. It reminded me of a quote from Albert Hoffman, the "father of LSD," who died at the age of 102 in 2008. Dr. Hoffman, a chemist who first synthesized the chemical, gave an interview to the *New York Times* at the age of 99. He said a lot of amazing things in that interview ("Nearly 100, LSD's Father Ponders His 'Problem Child,'" January 7, 2006) but one in particular sprang to mind. "Outside is pure energy and colorless substance. All of the rest happens through the mechanism of our senses. Our eyes see just a small fraction of the light in the world. It is a trick to make a colored world, which does not exist outside of human beings." Dr. Hoffman's description aligned itself with my experience. I was inextricably bound up with the world, not separate from it. I had always thought the point of Buddhist meditation was to change something in my mind, to effect some kind of inner transformation, to peel away layers until I unearthed my real (no-) self. I was secretly operating with a belief that there was something wrong with me that needed fixing, that my 'self' was evidence of this, that if I meditated enough I would be cleansed. But now I had a glimmer of another way of looking at it all. No-self was not a state to be achieved, it was a testament to my embedded nature. No self apart from the world. The whole idea of going deep within to change myself seemed suddenly ludicrous. I felt like I already belonged. Walking through the New England countryside thinking, I felt light and happy. The dotted lines of the medical school diagram held me in their sway.

When I left the retreat the next morning, something stayed with me. I drove out early and made it to the highway by ten o'clock in the morning. I started to get hungry and stopped at a highway rest area, not the kind of place I ordinarily would feed myself from. The fast food restaurant there, a vaguely Italian establishment, was virtually empty. There were two local teenagers, a boy and a girl, working behind the counter. I could sense my own internal patterning—I would not normally make much eye contact and would treat them politely but at a great remove. But these were the first people I could talk to after a week of silence. "What can I eat here?" I asked them. "I'm just coming from a retreat and should probably have a vegetarian something." I smiled at them and looked them straight in the eye and their acned faces shone. They were full of love. "We'll make you a stir-fry with melted cheese," one of them said and ten minutes later they brought it over to me on a paper plate. It was delicious. I was grateful. The exchange made all of us happy for the time being. I could tell that, at least for the moment, the retreat had changed something in me. No longer staving off my own traumas, I was much more open. Instead of remaining an obstacle, my mind was allowing me to connect.

The Buddha did not teach the four foundations as a ladder toward the sublime. That would have reinforced the tendency toward dissociation that his childhood memory encouraged him to give up. He taught them as a means of connecting people to their own humanity, much as I found that morning on the highway. While he did encourage beginning with mindfulness of the body and progressing through feelings to the mind, he also taught that all four foci existed simultaneously and that to privilege any one of them over another reinforced a tendency toward clinging. And the Buddha suggested that the steady application of mindfullness could have a palliative, even a transformational, effect on the way we handle life's difficulties. In the stories that accompany his teachings he makes this abundantly clear.

There is one sutra, called the Splinter of Rock Discourse,* which describes this in very physical terms. When I first came upon it, I liked the title right away. What was the Buddha going to say about a splinter of rock? In it, the Buddha is surrounded by seven hundred *devas* (godlike beings who often found it edifying to hang around him) who praise him for his fortitude in enduring the pain of a splinter of rock lodged in his foot. "Not complaining at all," the sutra reads, the Buddha "endured the pain with mindfulness and comprehension. He lay on his right side on the great robe which was spread on the ground folded fourfold, with one foot slightly further than the other one on which it rested." I was struck by the image of the Buddha nursing a painful wound. Even though he was a Buddha, he still was subject to

---

* "Sakalika Sutta," SN1.38 in the "Saṁyutta Nikāya" ("The Connected Discourses of the Buddha")

pain. While I knew it was not a psychological wound, I could not help imagining that it might be. I read the concluding stanza avidly, curious about what advice he might give to his admiring audience of other-worldly beings.

"In this world, he who is conceited lacks self-control," the Buddha said. "He who abandons conceit, who has a tranquil mind, and who has wisdom is free from all existence. A forest-dweller leading a lonely life, if he practices mindfulness, can cross over the planes of existence where death prevails to the other shore." His well-chosen words certainly seemed to hold out hope for those who suffered emotional as well as physical distress. Someone leading a "lonely life" could cross over from the "planes of existence where death prevails" to another shore. There, lying on his robe on the ground, the Buddha was talking quite personally.

I closed the book for a moment the first time I read the sutra and paused to reflect. There seemed to be a hidden psychological teaching here. Despite the presence of a splinter of pain, it was possible to abandon conceit and practice mindfulness. I remembered a phrase I had scribbled down a number of times upon hearing it, over the years, from Joseph Goldstein. "It's not *what* you are experiencing that's important," Joseph would often say. "It's how you *relate* to it that matters." I always found this shocking—each time I heard it, I felt like I was hearing it for the first time. Splinters of pain did not have to be obstacles to awakening; they could become vehicles of it once the "conceit" that attaches to them is abandoned.

I thought again of the Buddha's early loss of his mother. Maybe the splinter of rock was not just a splinter of rock. Maybe it was a stand-in for all of the pain we can do nothing about. Whether or not this was actually true, I began to consider it as another example of the place where Buddha and Winnicott overlapped. Developmental trauma leaves us with feelings we cannot control, feelings that rise in the night, feelings that color our minds without our really knowing where they come from. The rush to leave those feelings behind, to pretend they are not there, only leaves us more in their sway. The Buddha was modeling a different approach in this little discourse. He was lying there showing the gods what it meant to be human.

The Splinter of Rock Discourse helped me with my own anxious feelings. I thought of them as like his splinter. Children who in one way or another lose their connection with their mothers or fathers seem to internalize their loss in some way, not as a thought, or even as a memory, but as a feeling. These "self-feelings," described by Winnicott in his list that included "falling forever, going to pieces, and losing all vestige of hope in the renewal of contacts,"[4] become the anxious and unstable foundations of the emerging self, the insecurities upon which identity is constructed. "It is a joy to be hidden," wrote Winnicott of the struggles of such children, "but disaster not to be found."[5]

Meditation often becomes a vehicle for being found, for bringing the splinters of rock, the internalized remnants of childhood traumas, into conscious awareness. As day-to-day thoughts and preoccupations become less dominant, the lurking feelings that tint the personality begin to emerge. These more primitive and emotionally tinged identifications, the ones Winnicott hailed as primitive agonies, lie beneath the surface of the mind and find ways of expressing themselves when given the chance. Therapists know this and are trained to let their encounters with patients expose the traces of these early experiences. The Buddha's Splinter of Rock Discourse suggests that something similar can happen in meditation.

When the Buddha spoke of making unworldly or nonsensual feelings an essential part of the foundation of mindfulness, he was making room for what psychotherapists like Winnicott would describe twenty-five hundred years later. There are feelings we carry in our minds, ones that are not dependent on our immediate sensory surroundings but ones that define who we think we are, that entangle themselves with our sense of personal continuity. Often such feelings come from an early place, so early that they were there before we were, before our selves were formed enough to hold or understand them. These feelings demand attention, even when we are at rest. Meditation, the Buddha discovered, can work with these feeling tones productively.

I had a chance to speak with Joseph Goldstein about all of this once. We were teaching together in a daylong workshop. I had spoken in the morning, outlining my ideas about the Buddha's loss of his mother, and he came in the afternoon. Given my questions to him, he spoke about his own experience of the mindfulness of unpleasant feeling. In his years of intensive practice, Joseph said, he had to deal with a lot of fear. Even as he trained himself to be mindful of it, he became aware that he was actually waiting for it to go away. His fear did not seem related to anything he was actually going through in his meditation—yet it filled his mind while he was sitting. It seemed to fit the definition of a nonsensual, unpleasant feeling, and Joseph did not like it, despite his attempts to be with it mindfully. He had a slight prejudice against it because of how unpleasant it was, and he was always hoping, in the back of his mind, even though he knew better, that he could manage to get rid of it. His fear was a recurrent presence, and it was not until he resolved, after years of doing otherwise, to treat it as if it would *never* go away—even if it were to kill him—that it began to actually inform his practice. Rather than pulling away from it just a bit, in a subtle form of dissociation, he learned to rest his awareness in its unpleasantness, making it into an actual object of meditation rather than treating it as an enemy. He used as an example a conversation he once had with his Burmese teacher about meditating while he had a headache. After Joseph complained to his teacher about how the pain was keeping him from meditating properly, the teacher rebuked him.

"You're missing a great opportunity," he said. "That kind of pain can be a wonderful object of concentration. It can really settle the mind."

"Your mother must have put you down to sleep before you were ready," I joked to him when I heard him describe the ongoing nature of his fear. His description of it had put me in mind of Winnicott's primitive agonies, of the ways in which babies who are not adequately held have the fear of falling forever. I was thinking that Joseph's fear in meditation must have been his version of something left over from infancy that had happened too early for his mind to make sense out of. Unworldly unpleasant feelings, in the Buddha's language, seemed to be another way of talking about the remnants of childhood trauma we carry in our unconscious. These feelings are not based exclusively on what is experienced through the five senses—there is a mental component that overrides and preserves the experience.

Joseph looked at me kind of funny. "My mother used to say that for the first three years of my life I just cried and cried," he said. "She felt like there was nothing she could do."

For me, this conversation with Joseph helped things fall into place. While he had never particularly tied his meditation fear to his childhood experience—working it through meditatively did not demand that he make this connection—it helped me give language to the stirrings of my own unconscious, language that calmed my mind enough to let me apply the foundations of mindfulness to my anxious feelings. It helped me treat my anxiety without shame, letting it come and go as part of the flow of feeling of which I was a part, while recognizing that I was, perhaps, being given a window into my earliest emotional experiences, not all of them pleasant ones. If my anxiety was like the Buddha's splinter of rock, then I might be able to learn to be with it as he had been, "not complaining at all, enduring it with mindfulness and comprehension." This is something I have taken directly into my work as a psychotherapist. People often come with fear or frustration or anger or pain that seems to have been there from the beginning. By recognizing that these feelings may well be remnants of infantile experience, I can help them attend dispassionately but with real interest. Rather than feeling besieged by or ashamed of such feelings, people can take ownership while at the same time not judge themselves so much for their discomfort. This attitude has proven very helpful. Many patients, troubled by these leftover feelings, criticize themselves for them. "Other people have it much worse," they say. "I should feel lucky that this is all I have to worry about." But the self-judgments only compound the problem. They perpetuate the malattunement that was the likely source of the discomfort. Once someone can treat his or her feelings like a splinter of rock some movement becomes possible.

Something similar applies in cases of big trauma, too. Those who have encountered incredible hardship or loss often feel that their experiences are singular. They believe that they, alone, have been hurt, and they judge themselves, or worry that other people will judge them, if they reveal what they are going through or have been through. They expect themselves to "get over it," or, at the very least, to protect other people from their distress. Attending to their feelings mindfully, with attunement and responsiveness but without judgment, often feels too threatening. The Splinter of Rock Discourse has something for these individuals, too.

When the Buddha taught the Middle Path, his vision was one of balance. Having reconnected with his own capacity for joy, with his spirit of vitality, he now had the poise and stamina, the ease of mind and the fortitude, to hold the unpleasant aspects of his psyche in his awareness. In Winnicott's way of thinking, this equilibrium is what unfolds in the therapy office, with the therapist re-creating the holding environment of the good-enough mother and the patient left with no other option than to slowly let in, or out, the un-worked-through unpleasantness of the past. In Winnicott's language, the therapist creates a holding environment, a field of awareness, that mimics that of the early parent-infant bond. It does not duplicate it, but it is close enough that a sense of safety is reestablished and one's defenses are allowed to relax. In the Buddha's experience, the relational aspects of Winnicott's therapy were collapsed into meditation. In his case, the capacity to make the mind into an object of mindfulness, to know the mind knowing, created a holding environment for the entire range of his emotional experience. To return to the metaphor of the sky so favored in the Buddhist tradition, the Buddha's recognition of the background presence of the luminous emptiness of awareness allowed him to hold the splinters of his emotional life in a new way. While the splinters did not disappear, they lost their special status. They could coexist with his knowing mind just as the clouds coexist with the sky. In discovering his knowing mind, the Buddha demonstrated that there is an ongoing rapport that continues, within the individual, long after he or she emerges from the infantile parent-child matrix. The relational capacity that begins in infancy when we are totally dependent on our caretakers endures. We have the ability to be both subject and object to ourselves, and this capacity of reflective self-awareness has the potential to enlighten us, to ease the burdens we all carry.

In the Buddha's self-analysis, and in his later teachings on mindfulness, we can see his relational self in action. It is as if he were reproducing the parent-infant dynamic internally but taking it to a higher level. Listen to one of today's foremost researchers on mother-infant rapport, Peter Fonagy, to have a sense of how close the parallels are. He uses the word "affective" in his writing in the place of "emotional," but he is talking about the same thing, about how babies are helpless in the face of the onslaught of their own feelings.

We suggest that the infant only gradually realizes that he has feelings and thoughts, and slowly becomes able to distinguish these. This happens mainly through learning that his internal experiences are meaningfully related to by the parent, through her expressions and other responses. These habitual reactions to his emotional expressions focus the infant's attention on his internal experiences, giving them a shape so that they become meaningful and increasingly manageable. . . . The parent who cannot think about the child's mental experience deprives him of the basis for a viable sense of himself. . . .

Within a secure or containing relationship, the baby's affective signals are interpreted by the parent, who is able to reflect on the mental states underlying the baby's distress. For this reflection to help the baby, it needs to consist of a subtle combination of mirroring and the communication of a contrasting affect. The nature of the object's mirroring may be most easily understood in the context of our description of the parent's pretend play with the child: thus, to contain the child's anxiety, the mother's mirroring expression will display a complex affect, which combines fear with an emotion incompatible with it, such as irony. . . . We believe that the infant is soothed (or contained) through much the same process.[6]

Fonagy is describing the way a parent helps a child make feelings tolerable. He is evoking the means by which an attentive parent creates a field in which feelings can be known. In his view, this is an ongoing process, in which the parent attends to what is going on in the child, reflects upon it, and interprets it for him. Young children or infants have no idea what their feelings are. They are moved by them and possessed by them, but their minds do not yet have the capacity to hold or symbolize or name or understand what is going on. For this they are totally dependent on the adults who care for them. Fonagy describes what he has found in his laboratory, where he and his colleagues have observed infants with their parents. The good-enough parent senses what is going on in her child and mirrors it back with a slight twist. She lets the child know that she knows what is happening and she lightens it a bit with her combination of ironic detachment and sensitive attunement. The parent knows that whatever is happening is not the end of the world. If the child is hungry, she will be fed. If she is wet, she will be changed. If she is tired, she will go to sleep. If she is anxious, she will be held. And in the meantime, when the child is still caught up in the feelings of distress, the parent soothes her with her words and gestures. When Winnicott wrote of the parental "holding environment," he was writing of this very phenomenon. In relating meaningfully to the child's distress, the parent, over time, develops the capacity of the child's mind to understand what feelings are and to deal with them. Fonagy's word for this is "mentalization."

The Buddha's therapy, as described in his Four Foundations of Mindfulness, involves much the same process. What the Buddha counsels, in a moment-to-moment way, is just the kind of attitude that Fonagy described in an attuned mother: Seeing things clearly—the mirroring aspect—but not treating things as *too* real. Giving the information back with a slight twist, with a bit of paradox. "For me," said the Thai teacher Ajahn Chah, pointing to the drinking glass he kept by his side, "this glass is already broken. Yet when I know this, every minute with it is precious." When he called the glass already broken, Ajahn Chah was striking the ironic note of the Buddhist perspective. Undercutting our perceptions of what is real, he created a space in which the traumatic facts of impermanence and insubstantiality could be known. His words created a holding environment in which we could understand for ourselves how something could be both broken and whole, intensely alive and yet, in the words of the Buddha's Fire Sermon, burning with the trauma of impermanence. And there was something ineluctably calming about seeing it this way. What he was saying was true, and we could tolerate it.

When the Buddha taught the Four Foundations of Mindfulness, he was charting the path to selflessness. When one sees that one's experience is but a conglomeration of raw data, one's conviction about one's identity is shaken. When one sees that awareness has a life of its own—that we can be aware of it, or it can be aware of us, or that it simply *is*—our notions of who or what we are begin to collapse. The possibility of no-self makes us look at ourselves differently. Nothing changes, but there is a twist. What we had formerly assumed was so solid and real now comes into question. Ajahn Chah might say the glass is already broken—another Buddhist teacher might just call it empty. Whatever words they use, they are replicating the emotional stance of the good-enough parent who soothes her child by both mirroring and slightly undermining his all-consuming distress. "You take yourself so seriously," she gently teases, holding the difficult feeling with her smile.

The Buddha, in recovering his capacity for nonsensual joy, learned that this joy was limitless. He found that if he got himself out of the way, his joy completely suffused his mindful awareness. This gave him the confidence, the stability, the trust, and the means to see clearly whatever presented itself to his mind. In the curious bifurcation of consciousness that meditation develops, where we can be both observer and that which is being observed, the quality of joy that he recovered did not remain an internal object. It was not only a memory or merely a feeling to be observed; it was also a quality of mind that could accompany every moment of mindfulness. The more he accepted the presence of this feeling and the more it toggled between being object and subject, the closer the Buddha came to understanding his true nature. Splinter of rock or no splinter of rock, the Buddha was figuring out how to relate.

9

Implicit Memory

Not long ago, while cleaning out my bookshelves, I came upon a videotape, a VHS cassette, that had slipped behind a layer of novels on an upper shelf. I wondered about it as soon as I found it; I had recently transferred all my home movies from minicassettes to DVDs, but this discovery was of a different size and make from the others. I ran quickly to watch the tape on my television, congratulating myself on not having thrown away my cassette player yet, and found myself face to face with a forgotten episode from my past. The scene was from 1986; it was recorded when my daughter was five weeks old by a friend of a friend whose house we were visiting in upstate New York. I had not given the tape a single thought since it was recorded— I'm sure I had just stuck the cassette on my bookshelf and never watched it—yet as soon as the images began to play it all became very familiar.

Or so I thought. The video, which I watched about twenty minutes of, ostensibly focused on my wife's nursing and our care of our baby daughter. But it also caught me acting in a peculiar way I never would have remembered on my own. As the tape unfolded, I began to squirm as I watched my younger self in action. My own conduct, faithfully recorded by the camera, alarmed me. It was like being transported back in time and being simultaneously in my body and observing it from afar. I could see the 1986 version of myself confidently doing his thing, but I could also see much more. There, in vivid display, incontrovertibly, I could see myself acting out a destructive pattern of behavior that I was clearly unaware of. I was shocked to see myself acting in this way, taken aback by the level of discomfort I could sense in myself and by the discomfort I was inflicting on those around me. I was clearly anxious, or angry, or anxious *and* angry, but I was also, quite apparently, not in touch with whatever was going on inside me. Nothing about the scene felt familiar as I watched; it was like seeing an alternative version of myself in a parallel universe. If I could have, I would have refused to even recognize it as me.

But there was no mistaking the scene. My wife looked every bit herself, a lovely postpartum glow animating her as she nursed. And I was definitely me, although there was clearly something strange going on. Were it not for the videotape, I doubt I would have ever been able to own this particular aspect of myself. The video gave me access to something that my own defenses had kept out of my conscious mind. It let me witness the way my own trauma spilled out unbeknownst to me, the way it ran through and colored my young daughter's early life while traumatizing my wife's entry into motherhood.

After passing the baby back and forth, about five minutes into the recording, my wife took out a little toy that would later come to be an important element in our world. It was called a "wiggle worm," an eight-inch-long, yellow, stuffed rattle with little green plastic triangles along the breadth of one side. Once, several years later, we left the wiggle worm in a taxi we had taken to the airport, and we had to track it down and retrieve it, an exhausting endeavor that spoke to the wiggle worm's central importance in all of our lives. This tape marked its first recorded appearance.

I watched as, very tenderly, my wife held the wiggle worm aloft in the gaze of our baby daughter. She had just finished nursing, and her extemporaneous play was redolent of the mother–infant bond. She made the wiggle worm dance and sing, very gracefully, very adroitly, her voice very fine and light. She was incredibly attuned to the baby, who followed her movements carefully with rapt attention, the toy hovering just within her field of awareness. Then, in the next moment, inexplicably and out of the blue, I grabbed the wiggle worm and began shaking it loudly and clumsily in my daughter's face. "Wiggle worm, wiggle worm!" I cried. Jumping around like a monster, I brandished the thing like a weapon. I was like a caricature of an adolescent big brother stepping on my sister's precious dolls. In the movie, my daughter looked confused and then scared. What was I doing?

Observing myself on the television, I was aghast. I am often impressed, when I see photographs of myself or see myself on film, by how tense I look. I want to look away. This was a similar feeling, but much more intense. The violence in my actions was hard to take. While I had no recollection of these events, when watching them unfold on the tape, I had some sense of what must have been happening for me when I began to act out my dance. I was vaguely embarrassed by the delicacy of my wife's treatment of the wiggle worm. She was making it too alive. It was mattering too much. I wanted to make my friends laugh, but I was also, not so subtly, making fun of my wife. Only in retrospect could I see how uncomfortable I must have been with her attention to my daughter, how jealous I might have been, how much I needed to run roughshod over her or claim the attention for myself. And only later could I make a connection between my actions and the nursing that was the ostensible subject of the tape. Seeing my behavior on the screen put me in mind of my anxious dreams on my retreat. In both situations it was as if I were being taken over by something outside my control. It was one thing to try to make sense of it coming up through my dreams and another thing to see it in such prominent and vivid display on film. I felt sorry for my wife and my daughter, both of whom seemed bewildered, and ashamed of myself. And I could see that I was, in the language of psychotherapy, *enacting* something that was completely outside my capacity for reflective self-awareness.

Psychotherapists have long recognized that people color their experience through the prisms of their own particular minds. When this happens in therapy, it is called transference—it becomes the therapist's job to help patients understand that the ways they are misperceiving the therapist contain clues about early traumas that are being reawakened in the therapeutic relationship. But it is not only in a therapeutic relationship that people are subject to transference; people act out unprocessed emotions all of the time: at work, with their loved ones, even when stuck in traffic or waiting on line at the store. Unresolved trauma waits at the gate of experience, looking for an opportunity to express itself. As I could see in the videotape of myself, however, there is a peculiar quality to this expression. It pours out unbeknownst to the person engaging in the behavior. It is *enacted* with remarkably little self-awareness. Even after the action is completed, one has little idea of what was being expressed. One of the fascinating things about reading the Buddhist scriptures is seeing how this tendency was described twenty-five hundred years ago. Not only did the Buddha act out his dissociated aggression in his ascetic pursuits but, once awakened, he became expert at recognizing and treating this tendency in others, in ways that anticipated the work of today's most experienced trauma therapists. He became adept at interrupting the unconscious perpetration of trauma from one person to the next.

It is interesting that *sati*, the word the Buddha chose for mindfulness, means "to remember." In his choice of this word, it is as if he already understood today's most recent thinking about how trauma encodes itself in the mind and body. While the remembering aspect of mindfulness is usually taken to mean "remembering to be aware of whatever is happening in the moment," there is another quality to it that relates more directly to the way trauma cleaves to our experience. Re-membering also connotes bringing that which is dissociated back into the self. It can mean rejoining, or becoming cognizant, in the sense of bringing something into consciousness that has been lurking outside awareness. In the case of trauma, this second meaning of remembering is especially relevant.

One of the distinguishing qualities of trauma is that it cannot be held in normal memory. Because the feelings associated with it are by definition unendurable, they never make it into the part of the brain that makes sense of emotional experience. Robert Stolorow describes it this way. Developmental traumas, he says, "derive their lasting significance from the establishment of invariant and relentless principles of organization that remain beyond the influence of reflective self-awareness or of subsequent experience."[1] The neural pathways on which these emotional currents run are based in the amygdala, deep in the brain, and they operate outside the influence of conscious thought. They can hijack the mind and blank out awareness, as my reaction to the wiggle worm made clear, so that it feels as if one is suddenly in the grip of something over which one has no control. Stolorow makes an interesting point about the impact of trauma, one that the Buddha's psychology also supports. Trauma takes us out of time. There is no past or future when one is overtaken by it; it is as if it were happening *now*. "Experiences of trauma become freeze-framed into an eternal present in which one remains forever trapped, or to which one is condemned to be perpetually returned through the portkeys supplied by life's slings and arrows,"[2] he says. The sense of one's own continuity, of what he calls the "stretching along between past and future,"[3] is collapsed by trauma. The traumatized individual lives outside time, in his or her own separate reality, unable to relate to the consensual reality of others. The remembering quality of mindfulness counters this tendency. It allows the experiences of trauma to come out of their frozen states and back into the warmth of time.

This is why the research on the parent-infant relationship is so relevant. In a good-enough setting, a parent helps her child metabolize feelings over time. She prevents them from becoming traumatic. Through her attention, with her subtle combination of mirroring and irony, she provides comfort and soothing and in the process helps a child know feelings from a place where they can be symbolized. She helps her baby give shape or texture to her emotions, helps make them safe, so that eventually the child can hold them for herself in her mind. In trauma, this process does not occur. Developmental trauma results when the primary caregiver cannot fulfill this function for a child. Other traumas result when a person, or his or her meaningful others, cannot do something similar. Brain scientists, in their efforts to understand memory, have illuminated the probable explanation.

There are at least two kinds of memory: implicit memory and explicit memory. Implicit memory is the kind we use when we learn to ride a bicycle or throw a ball. We do not have to consciously recall anything when we utilize it; it is just there in our bodies ready to be used. This kind of memory is handled in a deep part of the brain, away from the higher cortical centers that manage conceptual thought and conscious awareness. There is behavioral knowledge without conscious recall; the memory is called "procedural" or "sensorimotor." It is as if it were lodged in the body, outside what we normally think of as the mind. Implicit memory develops naturally before verbally based memory comes into focus. It is the only memory available in the first eighteen months of life and is the foundation not just of motor skills but of learning how to do things with others.[4] Much of what we think of as "relational knowing"—joking around, expressing affection, and making friends[5]—is based in this kind of memory. We know how to do it without thinking about it. It does not require deliberate attention or verbal processing, yet it is intrinsic to who we are.

Explicit memory, on the other hand, allows for conscious recollection. It is also called "narrative" or "declarative" memory, and is what we normally think of when we talk about remembering something. It is mediated by thought of one kind or another and has a quality of reorganization. Raw experience is sorted out and reformulated and given coherence by the mind. A process of symbolization, of which language is a tool, is employed. When a parent helps a child regulate her anxiety by reflecting back what is happening and making it more tolerable, she is setting the stage for this kind of second-order symbolization, for a flow between the implicit and the narrative. Explicit memory functions through reflective self-awareness—when we have this kind of memory, we know that we are aware. It is accessed through thought, not directly through the body.

Traumatic experiences, it is now understood, are held only in implicit memory. Therapists who work with posttraumatic stress disorder see versions of this all the time. The emotional reactions of fight or flight associated with a specific trauma live on in the bodies of traumatized individuals as if in an eternal present. The traumatic reactions are locked into place, ready for a threat the individual has already seen but not explicitly known. The defense of dissociation cements the memories in place in the part of the brain that normally stores behavioral knowledge. The trauma is never processed by the higher centers of the brain. It leaks out when reminders surface or when one's guard is down, and it is only accessible through the traces it leaves in the body or in unconscious memory. As Philip Bromberg has written,

"What a patient is able to hold and symbolize cognitively versus what he must hold without symbolic processing and must thereby enact is the key issue. What is *there* is going to be registered in some form or other, and some unprocessed aspect of it will be enacted."[6]

When I saw myself on the videotape twenty-five years after the fact, I could see that I was enacting some kind of unprocessed aspect of myself. Held in my implicit memory, it was being pulled out of me by something in that particular situation that was bypassing conscious thought. Seeing it all these years later, I could, with some reflection, grasp what might have been going on. My wife's play with the wiggle worm, in the context of breast-feeding my daughter in the first weeks of her life, was making me uncomfortable. It was hitting me in a place I could not tolerate and making me act out aggressively. Why? Winnicott, with his exquisitely sensitive descriptions of the dynamics of the mother–infant relationship, had an idea. Reading him, I could sense how much my wife's play with the wiggle worm embodied something I ostensibly valued but was also made anxious by. She was manifesting just that quality of mind that helps a baby navigate emotional experience without becoming traumatized. In witnessing her demonstration of it, my own trauma resurfaced and I enacted it once again.

"The mother (or part of mother) is in a 'to and fro' between being that which the baby has a capacity to find and (alternatively) being herself waiting to be found,"[7] Winnicott wrote, in a description of how a parent stops her child's feelings from becoming stuck in implicit memory. She is both a separate self (waiting to be found) and a potential space in which her self is suspended, making room for the baby to find her. In letting herself be that which the baby has a capacity to find, she puts herself into relief. The baby then has the admittedly illusory experience (although not illusory to the baby) of discovering her, an experience that is inherently creative. "In the state of confidence that grows up when a mother can do this difficult thing well (not if she is unable to do it), the baby begins to enjoy experiences. . . . Confidence in the mother makes an intermediate playground here, where the idea of magic originates, since the baby does to some extent *experience* omnipotence."[8] This is what my wife was facilitating for my daughter. She was showing how the wiggle worm could become a transitional object and she was beginning to endow it with the qualities of the breast. She was making a playground in which the wiggle worm, and by extension herself, was both already there and waiting to be found. In sensing her intentions, something in me must have rebelled. My reactive behavior manifested exactly the opposite approach, one that Winnicott warned against. As is often the case with trauma, I began to act out what I must have, in some way, experienced. My implicit memories were going straight to my actions. Only this time I was engendering more trauma, passing it along to those I loved most in the world in an endless cycle the Buddha called samsara.

Winnicott used the language of gender to illustrate two possible approaches a parent can take with a child. "The male element *does* while the female element (in males and females) *is*,"[9] wrote Winnicott. Two mothers, both breast-feeding, can look identical, but the experience of their infants can be radically different. In one, the baby can find the breast for herself and have the feeling of creating it; in the other, the breast finds the baby and the infant has to comply. In the first scenario, the good-enough one, the baby, while feeding or being held, actually becomes the breast for a time. In the other scenario, the breast is given at the behest of the mother and the baby has to adapt. Instead of space being created in which the baby can find the breast, the baby is given no agency and no choice. When it is time to eat, it is time to eat. "Either the mother has a breast that *is*, so that the baby can also *be* when the baby and mother are not yet separated out in the infant's rudimentary mind; or else the mother is incapable of making this contribution, in which case the baby has to develop without the capacity to be, or with a crippled capacity to be."[10]

For Winnicott, if early experience goes well, it provides the foundation of a stable sense of confidence. "We find either that individuals live creatively and feel that life is worth living or else that they cannot live creatively and are doubtful about the value of living,"[11] he wrote. "Compliance carries with it a sense of futility for the individual and is associated with the idea that nothing matters and that life is not worth living."[12] The trust engendered by the "breast that *is*" carries over and makes emotional development possible. Even after the rise of the ego and the emergence of the self, this "capacity to be" is crucial. If it is there, it makes for a fluid ego, one that can dissolve into nourishing experiences, give way to the creative impulse, and spontaneously erupt in joy. If it is not there, the ego becomes more "male" in nature: There is a reliance on "doing," a more rigid approach to everyday life, and a more uncomfortable relationship to the self. "The study of the pure distilled uncontaminated female element leads us to BEING, and this forms the only basis for self-discovery and a sense of existing (and then on to the capacity to develop an inside, to be a container, . . .). At risk of being repetitious I wish to restate: when the girl element in the boy or girl baby or patient finds the breast it is the self that has been found."[13]

When the Buddha taught mindfulness, he seemed to grasp much of what psychotherapists like Winnicott spelled out for us. In particular, in his treatment of unworldly or nonsensual feelings, the Buddha described how the traumas encoded in implicit memory could become objects of meditation, how they tend to surface when the female element of "being" is given preeminence in the mind. Mindfulness creates another version of the container Winnicott identified as the mother's most important gift to her child. By moving the ego to a neutral place of observation, giving the "male element" something to *do*, and then focusing on raw experience, an internal environment is created that mimics the early infant–mother relationship. Under the spell of this kind of attention, implicit memories are given opportunities to reveal themselves. Like the videocassette I discovered in the back of my bookshelf, meditation asks us to reexperience aspects of ourselves we would rather forget. The re-membering aspect of mindfulness, like the writing process I engaged in after watching myself on the video, creates a bridge between implicit and narrative memory. One begins to give name and form to one's inchoate feelings, to gather one's dissociative elements back into the self. This can be a humbling experience, but it can also be a relief. The troubling aspects of the self are a lot less troubling when held in the forgiving arms of one's own awareness.

I sensed a version of this happening through my own reflections on the wiggle worm. Meditating on my strange behavior while writing about it helped me see a distressed aspect of myself with less shame and more understanding. It also helped me take responsibility for similar actions in later family situations. In the events captured on the videocassette, I was acting out a traumatic residue. Confronted with my wife's unself-conscious display of her own female element, I manifested a caricature of the male archetype, revealing something about my mind that I, and the people close to me, have had to deal with. In vivid display, I manifested what today's researchers have also concluded. "The organization of mind comes to mirror, in part, the organization of earlier communicative processes."[14] The early parent–child environment, the balance between being and doing, lives on in the mind. Mindfulness offers an opportunity to see these patterns clearly. In seeing them, in bringing them into the domain of reflective self-awareness, there is a possibility of emerging from their constraints.

Choice emerges where before there was only blind and conditioned behavior.

One woman who has come to a number of my lectures and workshops over the years, whom I will call Eva, confided in me recently how hearing me equate the work of Winnicott with the practice of mindfulness has helped her with her own trauma. She described how she would be "blindsided" over and over again by what she came to understand was primitive agony hiding in her implicit memory. Unexpectedly, and with no conscious control, events in her relational life—an unanticipated rejection, a minor disagreement or an unwanted demand from her husband—would provoke an outburst of fear or anxiety that would completely destabilize her. Drawn to the practice of meditation, Eva was able to describe how the progression of mindfulness—from the breath to the body to the feelings to the mind—helped her deal with her history. "It's not like the trauma ever really goes away," she told me. But by using the breath as a central, and neutral, object of mindfulness she was able to give herself enough room to sometimes face the "unendurable" feelings when they arose, instead of simply being at their mercy. For Eva, the word "sometimes" was crucial. "What meditation gave me was the choice to be with the feelings *or not*," she told me recently. "When they get to be too much, I can come back to the breath and feel safe."

Eva's experience matched my own. She found that meditation, by providing auxiliary ego-support and a more neutral observing stance, opened up her memories and allowed conscious access to feelings she could only have previously enacted. But the ability to have a choice in the matter was critical. When those difficult feelings arose, which they would do sporadically and unpredictably both in and outside meditation, she could move back and forth between them and her breath as she saw fit. Over time, she could get to know her feelings bit by bit, but she had enough control to not be totally overwhelmed by them. This made her less vulnerable when her traumatized emotions were set off in daily life. They were not such a surprise, and her fear around them became more tolerable.

The Buddha, in his embrace of mindfulness, found a middle path between indulgence and dissociation. Spurred on by his childhood memory, he took himself out of an eternal present in which he was endlessly acting out feelings of self-denigration and reestablished a link with his personal history. He made remembering the centerpiece of his therapeutic method. In his careful elucidation of the Four Foundations of Mindfulness, he established the means by which implicit memories can be converted to narrative ones. The process is analogous to that which occurs between mother and infant. The memories of feelings are sensed in the body and known by the mind. A second-order symbolization is made possible. A narrative, although not necessarily a verbal one, is created. A picture is made, a representation established, a felt sense known. Feelings are brought out of the body and into real time and space. The boundaries and fortifications around them are pulled down as the ego surrenders its supremacy to the auxiliary function of mindfulness.

Winnicott did not know of meditation; he knew of psychoanalysis. He felt that the therapeutic situation in many cases reproduced and mimicked the early child-parent relationship, providing a second chance for unexplored trauma to resurface in an environment in which it could be experienced as if for the first time.

> There are moments, according to my experience, when a patient needs to be told that the breakdown, a fear of which destroys his or her life, *has already been*. It is a fact that is carried round hidden away in the unconscious. . . . In this special context the unconscious means that the ego integra-

tion is not able to encompass something. The ego is too im-
mature to gather all the phenomena into the area of personal
omnipotence.

It must be asked here: why does the patient go on being
worried by this that belongs to the past? The answer must be
that the original experience of primitive agony cannot get
into the past tense unless the ego can first gather it into its
own present time experience. . . .

In other words the patient must go on looking for the
past detail which is *not yet experienced*. This search takes the
form of a looking for this detail in the future.[15]

The key to Winnicott's thesis is his understanding that *experience* is healing and that certain pivotal events have, nevertheless, not
yet been experienced or remembered. In the scenario that he outlined,
the infant at first needs the mother to provide protective ego coverage
so that difficult emotions or difficult experiences become tolerable. If
the mother's absence or preoccupation precludes this protective coverage, the infant has nowhere to go. The very help that he needs to deal
with the lack he faces is unobtainable. Instead of learning about tolerable frustration, there is only intolerable, and unthinkable, anxiety.
But the child cannot process this situation alone. It never gets dealt
with. Often it is filed away but resurfaces later: a kind of prototypi-
cal posttraumatic stress disorder. The person becomes fearful or anxious or aggressive but does not know why. Winnicott believed these
ghosts were actually ancestors and that *awareness* was the key to
unlocking their influence. "The purpose of this paper is to draw attention to the possibility that the breakdown has already happened, near
the beginning of the individual's life. The patient needs to 'remember' this but it is not possible to remember something that has not yet
happened, and this thing of the past has not happened yet because the

patient was not there for it to happen to. The only way to 'remember' in this case is for the patient to experience this past thing for the first time in the present, that is to say, in the transference. This past and future thing then becomes a matter of the here and now, and becomes experienced by the patient for the first time. . . . This is the equivalent of remembering."[16]

A person in therapy uses the therapist in much the same way that an infant uses a parent, as a provider of protective ego coverage, so that feelings that would otherwise be too frightening can be slowly passed back and forth and made known. Meditation, as the story of the Buddha's life makes clear, does something similar. It also creates a holding environment in which unknown and unexamined aspects of the past can be experienced for the first time in the here and now. My vision of myself on the videotape, like my dreams on retreat, gave me another opportunity to turn my implicit memories into narrative ones. Winnicott, who liked to frame things as "male" or "female," would have seen my predicament as emblematic of too much "male" energy. For him, there needed to be a balance between doing—the male element—and being—the female element. In my fight against doing and being done to, I was locked into a dissociated aggressive response. In search of attunement and responsiveness, I was nevertheless vulnerable to my own aggression. In the face of my wife's nursing of my daughter, I could not contain myself. Not only did I enact my own trauma, I created trouble for them.

The Buddha dramatized a version of this as he journeyed toward his enlightenment. The events that unfolded after the recovery of his childhood memory and the abandonment of his ascetic practices brought him face to face with the childhood trauma he had not yet fully experienced. In Winnicott's formulation, it had not yet happened because he had not been there enough for it to happen to him. But with his mind rejuvenated by his childhood memory and his body replenished by the offering of the maiden Sujātā, Gotama was ready to make more room for himself. Emerging from between the rock and the hard place that had so constricted him, he was poised to remember that which he had no conscious recollection of. The first sign of this came in the form of five great dreams. While they are traditionally viewed as prophetic, these dreams seem as related to the past as they do to the future. They suggest that the Buddha, like the rest of us, needed to connect with his history. With no videotape to come to his aid, his implicit memory yielded up its treasures in the only way it could. His dreams, as Freud would later confirm, were the royal road to his unconscious.

10

Dreams of the Buddha

nce, when asked, "Who are you?" by a bedazzled admirer, the Buddha replied simply, "I am awake." This famous statement is often misinterpreted. While it speaks of his uncovering of the Four Noble Truths—of suffering, its cause, its relief, and the path to its release—it can make it seem as if the Buddha never slept, as if he never dreamed, as if perpetual alertness was his main attribute. The Buddha was certainly awake, but he was not on guard. He was attentive to all who came his way, alert to their traumas and to their reluctance to admit to their traumas, and he was equally attuned to himself. In awakening to his true nature, the Buddha did not neglect the reality of those around him. A concern for others defined his attention.

One of the most important steps in the Buddha's awakening came in his sleep. Right after remembering his childhood joy under the rose-apple tree, after taking his meal of rice pudding and being abandoned by his five former friends, after throwing his begging bowl into the river and watching it float upstream, he had a series of dreams. They are recorded in one of the original collections of Buddhist sutras*

---

* *Aṅguttara Nikāya (Book of Gradual Sayings)*

but have been given scant attention over the years. The dreams were catalytic for the Buddha's growth and development. Not only did they reveal much about his own history of trauma, about who he was before his enlightenment and what he had to recover to get there, but they helped open him to a dormant capacity of his mind, one that he was then able to use to help others with their suffering. In dreaming himself into wakefulness, the Buddha remembered, and took possession of, a quality of human relatedness he had all but ignored previously. It was this recovery that made his enlightenment possible.

Dreams are dissociative by definition. They occur when the rest of the mind is shut down, and they allow difficult feelings to be expressed in symbolic form. In most cases, they are forgotten upon awakening or remembered only in bits and pieces, the forces of dissociation keeping the feelings disguised and away from waking consciousness. This was not the case for the Buddha at this crucial time in his life. In the process of turning his mind around, he became ready to face something he had been estranged from, and he needed his dreams to help him.

The Buddha remembered his five dreams and recorded them for posterity; he may even have been aware of them as he slept. The dreams put something to rest in the Buddha while also waking something up. They took away his need to *enact* his dissociated feelings, as he had done in his years of ascetic self-abasement, and they lucidly revealed something about himself he had been ignoring. Simply speaking, they showed him that he could be kind. In his years of spiritual searching he had perfected all kinds of esoteric talents. He could take his mind into spheres of nothingness, go for days and weeks without eating, and rend his flesh with the best of them, but he was still operating with barely disguised contempt, not benevolence, toward himself and his world. When the enlightened Buddha told his admirer that he was awake, it was this basic kindness he was pointing to. With the help of his dreams, he had awakened to his true nature, and his true nature, to his utter surprise, was a relational one.

The passage in the sutras that portrays the Buddha's dreams is an interesting one. It begins by describing him as "not yet wholly awakened" but as a "being awakening" to whom there came "five great dreams."[1] The idea that there was a period in the Buddha's life when he was in the *process* of awakening is special in itself. It is not universally accepted in Buddhist circles that such an intermediate period existed. There are whole schools of thought that have grown up around the idea of "sudden enlightenment" and others that defend a "gradual" one. But here is a clear reference to something in between. A special time in the Buddha's life when he was *awakening* and one in which his struggle to awaken occurred while he was dreaming. The relationship of this to the movement from implicit to narrative memory is interesting. The Buddha's awakening rested on his dream life, on a creative transformation of that which was lurking in his unconscious memory, on his ability to bring something unknown into awareness, to give it a narrative structure that could allow him to hold it in conscious self-reflection. This happened after his childhood memory, in which the Buddha began to take feelings seriously. Feelings led him to dreaming. And dreaming showed him how to relate.

The five dreams are all of a piece. They begin with one that immediately equates the awakening Buddha with an infant lying on his mother's body, and they proceed to paint a developmental picture of the emergence of an interactive self. While the dreams are traditionally thought to foretell the future, they quite specifically evoke the Buddha's dissociated past. In narrative form they link the Buddha's solitary enlightenment, won by virtue of his own individual effort and intelligence, to a recovery of the interpersonal foundations upon which his emergent self depended. The dreams make clear that awakening was possible only when the Buddha's inherent capacity for interpersonal relatedness could suffuse the entirety of his mental life.

As the sutra describes:

Just before the Perfect One, accomplished and fully enlightened, attained enlightenment, five momentous dreams appeared to him. What five? While he was still only an unenlightened Bodhisatta, the great earth was his couch; Himalaya, king of mountains, was his pillow; his left hand lay in the Eastern Ocean, his right hand lay in the Western Ocean, his feet lay in the Southern Ocean. This was the first dream that appeared to him, and it foretold his discovery of the supreme full enlightenment.

While he was still only an unenlightened Bodhisatta, a creeper grew up out of his navel and stood touching the clouds. That was the second dream that appeared to him, and it foretold his discovery of the Noble Eightfold Path.

While he was still only an unenlightened Bodhisatta, white grubs with black heads crawled from his feet to his knees and covered them. This was the third dream that appeared to him, and it foretold that many white-clothed laymen would go for refuge to the Perfect One during his life.

While he was only an unenlightened Bodhisatta, four birds of different colours came from the four quarters, and, as they alighted at his feet, they all became white. This was the fourth dream that appeared to him, and it foretold that the four castes . . . would realize the supreme deliverance when the Dhamma and the Discipline had been proclaimed by the Perfect One.

While he was still only an unenlightened Bodhisatta,

he walked upon a huge mountain of dirt without being fouled by the dirt. This was the fifth dream that appeared to him, and it foretold that although the Perfect One would obtain the requisites of robes, alms food, abode, and medicine, yet he would use them without greed or delusion or clinging, perceiving their dangers and understanding their purpose.[2]

The dreams themselves are amazing, and the traditional interpretations neat, lyrical, and inspiring. But the emotional nature of the dream content is worth paying attention to as well. It does not seem as if the traditional interpretations, pointing toward the future, quite do justice to the dreamer's emotional experience, linking him to his own personal history. In the first dream, for example, the sleeping Buddha is one with the universe. He is quite literally dreaming an oceanic feeling, with the mountains his pillow, the earth his couch, and his floating limbs supported by the water. He may well have been foretelling his enlightenment as the traditional commentaries suggest, but he was also telegraphing his recovery of the feminine, of his maternal aptitude. The earth as mother, the oceans as amniotic fluid, and the couch as her lap: These symbols would have evoked a maternal presence long before the advent of Freud. The Buddha's dream was not just predicting the future; in its depiction of the redolence of the present moment it was also recalling the past. His memory of childhood joy had opened him to being, and it appeared to him in his dream in the symbolic form of the earth and its waters as mother.

As if to prove the point, the Buddha's second dream literally grows from his navel. Vines creep to the sky, connecting him to the clouds and, by inference, to the heaven realm in which his mother took refuge after her death. If, as the traditional commentary suggests, the dream is predicting the discovery of the Noble Eightfold Path, it is doing so by revealing that the path to awakening does not involve withdrawal from the world but affirms a profound connection with it. The vines entwine the Buddha with the universe. They grow from his navel, reestablishing his original connection with his mother and re-affirming the primacy of his relational nature. The simultaneity of difference and connection, of separateness and unity, is painted by the image. The awakening Buddha is dreaming of the connectedness that emerges when one's primitive agonies are resolved, of the relatedness that takes the place of self-pity, of the inherently engaged nature of the self. He is dreaming of selflessness while revealing that there is no self apart from the world.

The third dream is the most mysterious. White grubs with black heads crawling from his feet to his knees. To me, the grubs are like Winnicott's primitive agonies or Eigen's broken dreams: the leftover remnants of childhood experience that make our skin crawl. They make me think of the ascetics of the Buddha's time, dedicated to self-mortification, and of the many people of our own time, tormented by self-hatred, who are as devoted to psychological self-mortification as those of the Buddha's time were to the physical. The grubs are sinister, like maggots in the flesh of the ancient ascetics, but also redemptive, like cicadas, which in Japan represent rebirth, crawling as they do from the ground every summer to fill the air with their distinctive background song. In this imagery, the Buddha's third dream aligns his awakening with therapists' insights about aborted emotional experience. The dream suggests that agony, like the white grubs with black heads, can be a vehicle of awakening and that the broken aspects of our being have within themselves the template for wholeness. Each person who came to the Buddha brought his own individual anguish along, and each such person, in harnessing his capacity for remembering, let that anguish crawl upward.

I thought of this dream during a workshop I was teaching a little while ago. A handsome young man was sitting all the way in the rear of the room, twenty or thirty rows back. He was one of only a few African Americans in the workshop, a man of about thirty, confident in his bearings. He wore a knit cap on his head and commanded the attention of all as he spoke. "I've been struggling with something all day," he began. "When I meditate now, I am filled with a feeling of loss. It has to do with my father, who left when I was young. There's a lot of anger, and I can feel myself wondering if it was my fault, even though I know that's ridiculous. But when I stay with it more, I just feel it turning into a kind of deadness: a lethargy, as if nothing matters. I feel myself sinking into the feeling and it feels dangerous, as if life has been stripped of meaning. What would you suggest?"

I was struck by his sincerity and his courage in speaking of something so personal in front of such a large group. I could feel him missing the father he hardly knew and turning that pain against himself, as if he were broken or cursed. I thought of the Buddha's loss of his mother and of the process of recovery that his dreams signified. And I remembered how the Buddha, like this man, first sank into nothingness and then willed himself toward deadness. His third dream, in which there is some kind of creative emergence from the grubby ground, gave me the inspiration to respond.

"These feelings of rage and distress and despair that you talk about," I said, circling something I knew I would have trouble articulating. "They only exist because of your original love for your father. They are like signposts back to that love. His leaving took that love with him, or appeared to, but you will see, if you stay with your meditation, that all of that love is still there in you. From the infant's perspective, it's directed at only one or two people, but even if they failed you, that capacity for love is still there in you. It's too bad for your father that he didn't get to know it—but there are plenty of people now who will be grateful for it. There's a whole roomful right here."

There was a danger of glibness in my response, but I think the gentleman in the workshop felt the intention of my words. While they were framed around notions of love, they were also drawn from our discussions of Buddhist and Western psychology. As long as he was locked into the self-image of being a fatherless child, cut off from the one whom he needed, this man was caught in his presumed identity. He was aware of his trauma, but he was using it to distance himself from life. He had a story about himself but no access to who he might have been before his trauma derailed him. I was trying to use his feelings of deprivation as a means of bringing him back in touch with a more fundamental truth about himself, to guide him back toward—or at least help him to visualize—the intrinsic relational foundation of his being. By not fighting with his internal wounds, by not insisting on making them go away, by not recruiting everyone in his intimate life to save him from his feelings of abandonment, by simply resting with them the way we do in meditation, he could learn, as the Buddha did, that he already was the love he thought he lacked.

The fourth dream, of the four birds coming together as one, speaks of the sense of internal cohesion that comes when the self is no longer held hostage by the traumas of childhood or the conflicts of adult life: When the self, in all of its multiplicity, is known as one. The four birds of different colors, reflective in the traditional accounts of the four castes in Indian society, are also suggestive of dissociation and estrangement. However it may be conceived, the traumatized self is fragmented, divided into parts, unable to hold the entire range of its history. Experience is constricted because the full range cannot be tolerated. The ground for holding it is not strong enough.

One association comes to mind in reference to this fourth dream of the Buddha. It has to do with a patient of mine who suffered a terrible loss of multiple members of her family in a tragic accident. Several years afterward, she began to write of the life she had lived. She wrote a series of remarkable pieces, each one redolent of one of her deceased family members or of an earlier time with them. The actual writing put her into an almost hypnotic reverie in which the reality of the lost time was more vivid than the one she was now living in. Each piece of writing was a bit of recovery that made her feel less lost herself. But after composing each piece, she was for a long time unable or un- willing to read any of them over. Each fragment of her life had its own reality, but the totality of her loss was too much to bear at any one time. The Buddha's dream, of the four birds coming together as one, speaks to my patient's predicament. It was a difficult thing to bring those fragments together. For a long time she could not.

The Buddha's fifth dream evokes both the extraordinary and the ordinary nature of his achievement. He walks on a mountain of dirt and is not fouled by it. Note that the dirt is not transformed into gold or anything. It stays dirty. But the Buddha, astride his pile of dirt, is untouched by it. This is another version of the third dream, in which that which was seen as a barrier to awakening is now known as the foundation upon which it rests. Enlightenment does not mean getting rid of anything; it means changing one's frame of reference so that all things become enlightening. The unity of the Buddha's experience is emphasized in this dream; he is not dividing himself into worthy and unworthy pieces; he is one being, indivisible, immune from the ten- dency to double back and beat up on himself. He has seen the worst in himself and not been taken down.

All five of the Buddha's dreams make this point. Rather than in- completeness or interruption, he is dreaming tolerance and wholeness. All of his previous efforts to eliminate the dirt from his being were overkill. What he found, instead, in his discovery of the Middle Path, was an incredible balancing capacity. He need not sleep on a bed of nails, nor walk on water; he could simply rest in his own skin without picking at it. That his dreams showed him this capacity in imagery steeped in the mother–infant bond speaks to the essential relational nature of his awakening. The same themes that Western therapists describe between mother and infant found their mature expression in the Buddha's self-analysis.

Before his turnaround under the rose-apple tree, the Buddha was in rebellion against being. He was trying to extinguish it by any means possible, using all of his masculine energy to subdue, control, and conquer his body and soul. The ideology behind this effort was one of master and slave. Being was thought to obscure spirit. One could find God by squeezing out the life energy or by rising above it. This was the motivation behind virtually all of the Buddha's preenlightenment efforts. After his memory, his whole approach changed. No longer driven by self-hatred and no longer exclusively identified with being the *doer*, the Buddha became able to give himself room. He opened the playing field and became curious about what was there. His dreams heralded the recovery of his female element, the emerging freedom of his creative capacities, and the reestablishment of the maternal holding environment from which he had become estranged. He could now reach inside and dream.

The Buddha, in summoning imagery of his long-forgotten mother, not only dreamed the origin of his trauma but also dreamed the means of its release. As I tried to explain to the gentleman in my workshop, the acknowledgment of personal agony sometimes connects a person to who they were before they were traumatized. This seems to have been the case for the Buddha. His five dreams, taken together, paint a picture of the recovery of what is today called "implicit relational knowing."[3] This is a form of "collaborative communication"[4] with deep roots in early life that researchers have identified as the most important bulwark against developmental trauma.

In implicit relational knowing, there is a nonconscious flow of feelings between people that helps them know how to be with each other. This is the form of communication that infants and their parents rely upon before language. It is different from the reflective/verbal knowing that grows out of speech and it seems to be mediated by what brain scientists are now calling "mirror neurons." Mirror neurons are brain cells in the motor cortex that fire when one person sees another person do something. They mimic the observed behavior: They reflect it, so that the brain does not know if you are doing the action or if I am. They are vehicles of empathy, automatically tying people together, mixing up experience between self and other. When I see my baby grimace, my mirror neurons give me the immediate sensation of grimacing. I know what she is experiencing without having to think about it and, if I am positively engaged, I will automatically do something to help her. "The human brain cannot develop and sustain itself without relatedness, which is a continuously active condition of mental life,"[5] writes one contemporary researcher. "How well the infant-caregiver relationship maintains positive engagement and regulates the infant's fearful arousal will have escalating consequences."[6] Parents make use of implicit relational knowing to help their infants cope with difficult feelings. An attuned and responsive caregiver senses what a baby is experiencing and strives to make things tolerable. He does this not by thinking about it but by simply knowing and responding.

The Buddha's dreams put him back in touch with his own capacity for knowing. After reconnecting to the joyful and creative element encapsulated by his childhood memory, he found a maternal energy infusing his imagination in his dreams. He moved from a position in which he was a lonely, isolated individual struggling to subdue his unruly self to one in which he was irrevocably aware of the intrinsic relational backdrop of his being. Despite the early loss of his biological mother, he now saw his rootedness in relationship as primary. As Michael Eigen, one of the few contemporary psychoanalysts who does not shy away from the mystical aspects of the field, has described it, "If you penetrate to the core of your aloneness you will not only find yourself, there will also be this unknown boundless presence. Is it you? Is it other than you? What is it? An unknown, boundless presence at the very core of your aloneness. No matter how deep you go, you'll find it there."[7]

The Buddha's dreams, envisaged when he was awakening, reveal his version of this unknown, boundless support. Coming on the heels of his memory, they are evidence of his psyche in upheaval. No longer driven by an ideology of subjugation, the Buddha can be seen in the process of reconfiguring himself. What is most apparent in the dreams is the opening up of his self. It is as if all the doors and windows are thrown ajar. The sun and the wind and the waters and the earth and the birds and the plants and even the bugs and dirt come streaming in. The lonely, isolated individual struggling with the feelings of being an ill-fitting axle in the wheel of life suddenly finds himself supported by the very world that was heretofore felt to be threatening. And this happens through the depiction in narrative memory of the connection with his mother that he had previously been unable to acknowledge or articulate.

The Buddha's mother, an enlivening presence stripped away before she could be really known, pervades his dreams and becomes the substrate of his enlightenment. She imbues his imagination and, in so doing, returns to him a capacity for relating in a maternal way. The Buddha's genius lay in his ability to take this capacity, newly returned to his mind, and deploy it in his spiritual search. He took the hint from his dreams and used it to balance his striving. Out of his implicit memory he found the female element he needed to make a stable path for himself. A comment from the artist Marcel Duchamp makes clear that this opening of a channel from implicit to narrative memory can have just this quality of joyful recovery. "Art cannot be understood through the intellect," wrote Duchamp, "but is felt through an emotion presenting some analogy with a religious faith or a sexual attraction—an aesthetic echo. The 'victim' of an aesthetic echo is in a position comparable to that of a man in love, or of a believer, who dismisses automatically his demanding ego and, helpless, submits to a pleasurable and mysterious constraint. While exercising his taste, he adopts a commanding attitude. When touched by the aesthetic revelation, the same man, in an almost ecstatic mood, becomes receptive and humble."[8]

The Buddha, before his aesthetic echo, was in the classic position of a traumatized individual acting out dissociated feelings without knowing what was being expressed. In his renunciation of desire, as enacted first in his abandonment of his wife and child and then in his ascetic practices, he was expressing the same "loss of faith in human relatedness"[9] that children with developmental trauma also show. Clinical studies of such children reveal that a preponderance of them have parents who have related to them in either a helpless and fearful way or a hostile and self-referential one. The children of helpless and fearful parents, in particular, have a very difficult time later in life. Their parents tend to be sweet and fragile, not hostile or aggressive, but they exhibit much more "apprehension, hesitation or withdrawal"[10] in response to their children's overtures than other parents. While they give in to their infant's entreaties eventually, they "often hesitated, moved away, or tried to deflect the infant's requests for close contact before giving in."[11] The children of such parents, researchers have found, become increasingly disorganized and defeated as they grow. They feel invalidated, as if crucial aspects of their experience do not matter. They use dissociative strategies to cope with their difficult feelings rather than turning to their uncomfortable parents for help, and they often resort to one of two interpersonal coping strategies by the age of three to five. In the first, termed a controlling-caregiving strategy of attachment, they find some way of taking care of the parent in lieu of being taken care of themselves. In the second, termed a controlling-punitive strategy, they garner a parent's attention by "entering into angry, coercive, or humiliating interactions with the parent."[12] The controlling nature of both of these strategies makes satisfying later relationships much more difficult to achieve.

If the tendency in Buddhist culture to diminish the import of the Buddha's early loss of his mother can be taken as reflective of his own early experience, then we can assume a kind of invalidation at the heart of the Buddha's being. While his family, like the culture in general, may have been eager to make it seem as if it did not matter that his mother had died, the young child may have been consistently given a message that his deepest feelings had no foundation in reality. This could account for his self-reported "delicate" nature. The family's helpless and fearful attitude could have easily been internalized, obscuring the more complex mix of emotions that might be expected.

The Buddha's dreams show him to be healing himself through the very dissociative defenses he must have once used to cope with his trauma. But instead of those defenses cutting him off from imponderable agonies, they are now used to return a sense of unknown boundless presence. In letting the imagery of the mother move from implicit to narrative memory, as the Buddha did in remembering his dreams, his own implicit relational capacities, locked up and dissociated by the early trauma, could be set free. In demonstrating this, the Buddha was making an important example for the ages. For almost no one is exempt from trauma. While some people have it in a much more pronounced way than others, the unpredictable and unstable nature of things makes life inherently traumatic. What the Buddha revealed through his dreams was that, true as this may be, the mind, by its very nature, is capable of holding trauma much the way a mother naturally relates to a baby. One does not have to be helpless and fearful, nor does one have to be hostile and self-referential. The mind knows intuitively how to find a middle path. Its implicit relational capacity is hardwired.

There is a passage in a Buddhist book by Jack Kornfield, written in the aftermath of the Vietnam War, that shows how useful this meditative version of implicit relational knowing can be in the treatment of trauma. The passage describes the experience of a Vietnam veteran at a meditation retreat who finds himself confronted by memories of atrocities he witnessed while a soldier. While it is specifically about the trauma of war, it can also be read as a metaphor for any kind of disruptive emotional experience.

The passage begins with the traumatized veteran reminiscing about his time as a field medical corpsman with the Marine Corps ground forces in the mountains on the border between North and South Vietnam. He saw many people, both soldiers and civilians, killed and injured. For years after his discharge he had recurring nightmares at least twice a week about being back in the war zone, "facing the same dangers, witnessing the same incalculable suffering, waking suddenly alert, sweating, scared." [13]

After eight years, he attended his first meditation retreat and found, to his horror, that in the silence of the sanctuary his nightmares came to fill his waking consciousness as well. The peaceful California redwood grove in which the retreat was held became the scene of multiple wartime flashbacks redolent of the hospital, morgue, and battlefield of the war. It was not what he was expecting nor was it what he wanted. But he came to understand that he was finally experiencing emotions he had been unprepared for when he entered the Marines. This gave him some courage to stay with the feelings longer than he really wanted to.

"I began to realize that my mind was gradually yielding up memories so terrifying, so life-denying, and so spiritually eroding that I had ceased to be consciously aware that I was still carrying them around. I was, in short, beginning to undergo a profound catharsis by openly facing that which I had most feared and therefore most strongly suppressed." [14]

With encouragement from his meditation teachers, he also saw that he was afraid of what he was unleashing in himself. Having released the wartime images he was carrying in his unconscious, he became worried that he would now be at their mercy, plagued by them in day as well as by night. But what he found was just the opposite. While he did retrieve the horrible images, he rediscovered a lost innocence as well. The beauty of the jungle, the glistening white sands of the Vietnamese beaches, and the intense greens of the rice paddies at dawn all filtered back to him. Not only did he remember his trauma, he remembered himself *before* his trauma.

"What also arose at the retreat for the first time was a deep sense of compassion for my past and present self: compassion for the idealistic, young would-be physician forced to witness the unspeakable obscenities of which humankind is capable, and for the haunted veteran who could not let go of memories he could not acknowledge he carried."[15]

This newfound kindness, toward himself and his history, stayed with him after the retreat. It became a touchstone in his mind that accompanied his troubling recollections, robbing them of their sting. While his memories persisted, his nightmares did not. The last of them occurred while he was fully awake, sitting in silence in the meditation hall, the watchful gaze of a Buddha holding him in its sight.

When I read this passage at a recent talk, a therapist in the audience raised her hand. She was moved by the account and reassured in a fundamental way in terms of her own work. Although she was a trauma therapist, she was anxious about bringing such material, partially submerged or partially repressed, into her patients' awareness because of the fear of overwhelming them with their own feelings. She was a therapist burdened by all that she had heard, traumatized by trauma, dangerously close to burning out, who had a protective attitude toward her patients, for whom she clearly cared deeply. She was trying to protect them from themselves, however, and so was shouldering their traumas instead of helping them accept what had happened. She was missing, or had lost, the faith or confidence that something greater than trauma could emerge from the therapeutic process. And she was also, I thought, protecting herself from her clients' pain. Listening to the passage quoted above gave her a vision of what was possible, a vision of the connection both she and her patients were capable of, even in the face of tremendous personal suffering. While the example may seem extreme, its lesson is basic. When we stop distancing ourselves from the pain in the world, our own or others', we create the possibility of a new experience, one that often surprises because of how much joy, connection, or relief it yields. Destruction may continue, but humanity shines through.

A therapist colleague of mine, a professor at the New School for Social Research named Jeremy Safran, tells a personal story about an encounter with a Tibetan Buddhist lama that makes much the same point. In the epigraph of a book he edited about encounters between Buddhism and psychoanalysis, Safran describes an unexpected exchange with his accomplished teacher that puts me in mind of the Buddha's dreams. As Safran remembers, his Tibetan teacher, Karma Thinley Rinpoche, once asked him, "in his broken, heavily accented English," how Western psychology treats nervousness.

"Why do you ask?" Safran responded.

"Well," he replied, "I've always been a nervous person. Even when I was a little boy I was nervous, and I still am. Especially when I have to talk to large groups of people or to people I don't know, I get nervous."

It is best to let the rest of the story come directly from Dr. Safran:

As was often the case with the questions that Karma Thinley asked me, I found myself drawing a complete blank. Part of it

was the difficulty of trying to find the words to explain something to somebody whose grasp of English was limited, but
there was another more important factor. On the face of
it this was a simple question. But Karma Thinley was a highly
respected lama, now in his sixties, who had spent years mas-
tering the most sophisticated Tibetan Buddhist meditation
techniques. Those who knew Karma Thinley considered him
to be an enlightened being. In the West psychotherapists are
increasingly turning to Buddhist meditation as a valuable
treatment for a variety of problems including anxiety. Who
was I to tell him how to deal with anxiety? And how was it
possible that Karma Thinley, with all of his experience meditating could still be troubled by such everyday concerns? How
could an enlightened person be socially anxious? Was he really enlightened? What does it mean to be enlightened? My
head swirled with all of these inchoate questions, and for a
moment my mind stopped. I felt a sense of warmth coming
from Karma Thinley and I felt warmly towards him. I felt
young, soft, open and uncertain about everything I knew.[16]

When I first read this passage, I called Safran on the phone, even
though we did not really know each other. I thought it was a beautiful description of the state of mind that Buddhism encourages. I liked
the way the lama used his social anxiety to topple Safran's expectations
of him, and I appreciated the deeper message. Awakening does not
mean an end to difficulty; it means a change in the way those difficulties are met. "Young, soft, open and uncertain about everything I
knew." There was a recovery inherent in the passage, a recovery of
what Michael Eigen had called the unknown boundless presence at the
core of aloneness, of what Duchamp christened the aesthetic echo, of
what the Buddha found in his dreams. It is not only trauma that is

lodged in implicit memory: The intrinsic relational knowing at the heart of the infant-caregiver bond is hidden there too. The Buddha, in his wakefulness, brought it out of the shadows and let it fill his being. As rejuvenating as this was, in some sense the Buddha was just redis-covering the wheel. Parents the world over have been clued in to their own version of the Buddha's wisdom for ages. "It is an important part of what a mother does," wrote Winnicott in a description of how she handles an infant's rage at the discovery that she is not completely under his control, "to be the first person to take the baby through this first version of the many that will be encountered, of attack that is sur-vived. This is the right moment in the child's development, because of the child's relative feebleness, so that destruction can fairly easily be survived."[17] Like the Buddha, Winnicott knew that trauma was inevi-table, even for infants. A mother's ability to help her baby through it with kindness and care is what the Buddha remembered.

Safran told me he was grateful for my call. His publisher, a Buddhist press, had urged him to leave this passage out of the book. Like the Buddha in the immediate aftermath of his awakening when he despaired of anyone understanding him, the publisher felt it would be too confusing for the readers.

Reflections of Mind

When my father was dying from his brain tumor, I realized that I had never had a conversation with him about anything spiritual. He was a scientist and, while he was proud of my success as a writer, he never expressed any real interest in the kinds of things I was thinking about. I was reluctant to engage him in too much discussion, knowing that he was not interested, and that seemed fine with him. When it became clear that his malignant brain tumor was inoperable, however, and that his days were severely numbered, I began to wonder if I shouldn't try to talk to him about what I had learned from Buddhism. This was a challenge, not because of his tumor, which was deep in the right side of his brain and had not affected his cognitive abilities, but because I needed to find a way of talking to him in plain language, without recourse to concepts he did not believe in. I called him on the phone from my office, not knowing that several days later he would slip into a coma from which he would never emerge, an unintentional infection from a brain biopsy several weeks previously taking its iatrogenic toll.

As I mentioned at the beginning of this book, my father, although a physician, successfully avoided the subject of his own mortality for much of his life. This is not an uncommon strategy for dealing with death, and there are many sutras in the Buddhist canon that show the Buddha confronting it with whatever persuasiveness he can muster. In one such sutra, known as the Simile of the Mountain, the Buddha asked a local ruler, King Pasenadi, how he would feel if a huge mountain were to come bearing down on him from the east, crushing all living beings in its path. He conjured the mountain expertly, making the king imagine a gigantic mass moving inexorably toward him, rolling over all things. Then he repeated the question but had the mountain coming from the north, then the south, and finally the west. By the time he was finished, the poor king, ostensibly secure behind his fourfold fortifications of elephants, chariots, cavalry, and infantry, was being crushed from all sides. This is what death is like, the Buddha trumpeted. It's coming, you don't know from which direction, and you are powerless to stop it. He seemed almost gleeful.

Why was this such a profound teaching for the king? Even now the words retain their threatening power. Don't we know all this already? Is death really such a surprise? The Buddha suggested that we do not really know it, even though we may mouth the words. The tendency toward denial runs very deep. We don't actually think it can happen to *us*. Or rather, we can't actually *imagine* it happening to us. The Buddha's incantation brought the reality home, at least for an instant, for King Pasenadi. The king inclined his mind toward the truth, brought it into his explicit awareness, and became receptive to the Buddha's teachings.

One of the most obvious reasons for avoiding the reality of death is that we do not know how to deal with it. The Buddha, in helping King Pasenadi see the impotence of his fortifications, was making this very point. We think we have to erect barriers to it or find weapons to fight it, but this does not work very well. The Buddha discovered a softer approach, one that he was urging the king toward. In his recovery of implicit relational knowing, as personified in his five great dreams, he found the key to navigating the inevitable traumas of life, including that of death.

My father already had the mountain on top of him. He had worked until he was eighty-four, until he got lost one day driving the same ten-minute route home from work that he had taken for the past forty years. The mountain, in the form of the tumor, was already inside his brain. As he was not used to facing a challenge he could not overcome with his intelligence, there was an air of resignation hovering over this, our last conversation.

"You know the feeling of yourself deep inside that hasn't really changed since you were a boy?" I began. "The way you have felt the same to yourself as a young man, in middle age, and even now?"

My father voiced his assent. I was trying to summon the place of intrinsic relational knowing for him. It is there, in our own subjectivity, although it is difficult to describe. We know ourselves from the inside: We have an intuitive feel for ourselves that is outside thought. And we relate to other people, indeed to the world, from this place. Most of the time, in our active and harried lives, we gloss right over it, but it is there in the background and we return to it in our private, unscripted, moments: when listening to music, taking a walk, or going to sleep, for example. In my mind I was remembering one of my Buddhist teachers asking me to find "what" (not "who") was knowing the sounds I was hearing when I was meditating. "Can you find what is knowing?" he would often question, as I turned my attention to the sounds of the meditation hall. The very effort to find "what is knowing" (although it was impossible to find) opened up a peaceful oasis of calm awareness in which I learned to abide. "Even though we can't find what is knowing, knowing is there," my teacher would say. This affirmation was a traditional Buddhist way of bringing implicit relational knowing into explicit awareness. "Knowing is there." It was impossible to refute.

My father, as best as I could gather, seemed to understand what I was getting at.

"It's kind of transparent, that feeling," I went on. "You know what it is, but it's hard to put your finger on it. You can just relax your mind into that space, though. The body comes apart but you can rest in who you have always been." Death is like taking off a tight shoe, I wanted to tell him, but I wasn't sure he would believe me if I went that far in the conversation. Yet I thought, with his scientist mind, he might just sense the possibility of investigating what I was suggesting. If the Buddha was to be believed, there was a place of lucidity from which even dying could be observed.

"Okay, darling, I'll try," he replied. I wondered for an instant if he was being patronizing but decided he was not. He often called me darling, and I was glad for it, in the end.

The stance I was suggesting to my father was akin to what the Buddha found in his dreams, the one that parents use to know what their infants are going through, that infants use to sense their parents' attunement, and that people continue to use to relate to one another empathically. This implicit relational knowing is immediate. It operates independently of language and opens a window into what is. It oriented us at the beginning of life, when our parents were our major lifelines, and it can be accessed even in death. The Buddha found that it was critical to his process of awakening and he deployed it, just as I hoped my father might, not only when he was dying but in his final struggle for enlightenment. Implicit knowing usually takes place outside awareness. It is generally nonconscious, operating on its own neurological pathways. Buddha found a way of resting the mind in its true relational nature, of bringing implicit awareness out of the darkness and making it conscious. As dramatized in the story of his enlightenment, he then discovered that old patterns of reactivity, stored as they are in implicit memory, could be deactivated when held in the light of unspoken knowing. Under the rubric of bare attention and mindfulness of mind, this became the fulcrum of the Buddha's method of mental development.

In his recovery of implicit relational knowing, catalyzed by his childhood memory and elaborated in his five great dreams, the Buddha found the key to navigating the inevitable traumas of life and death. He did not make his method up out of the blue; it was already there in embryonic form in his mind, hidden away in the vestiges of the earliest relationship of his life, but the Buddha had to go through a lengthy process to rediscover it. Buddhist masters ever since have had to come up with creative ways of communicating the simple bearing I was trying to help my father find. Its very simplicity often makes it difficult to grasp. The Thai forest master Ajahn Chah, whose metaphor of the glass as already broken so captivated me when I first heard it, had a particularly clear way of conveying it. In describing the Buddha's method of evenly suspended attention—in which all phenomena, be they pleasant, unpleasant, or neutral, are related to without clinging or condemning—he gave a wonderful description of the stance the Buddha learned to deploy.

> In our practice, we think that noises, cars, voices, sights, are distractions that come and bother us when we want to be quiet. But who is bothering whom? Actually, we are the ones who go and bother them. The car, the sound, is just following its own nature. We bother things through some false idea that they are outside us and cling to the ideal of remaining quiet, undisturbed.
>
> Learn to see that it is not things that bother us, that we go out to bother them. See the world as a mirror. It is all a

reflection of mind. When you know this, you can grow in every moment, and every experience reveals truth and brings understanding.[1]

Ajahn Chah framed his discussion in terms of the minor irritations that arise in silent meditation: the bothersome noises, sights, and distractions that make meditation challenging, but he was also, by implication, talking about the major irritations of old age, illness, and death. When he said that *every* experience reveals truth and brings understanding, he was not excluding the most traumatic ones. For Ajahn Chah, the ability to see the world as a mirror, to relate to it with the attunement, engagement, and care that a parent naturally showers upon an infant, was the greatest accomplishment.

In his teachings on the Foundations of Mindfulness, the Buddha laid out his perspective in starkly beautiful terms. "Monks," he said, "this is the direct path for the purification of beings, for the surmounting of sorrow and lamentation, for the disappearance of *dukkha* and discontent, for acquiring the true method, for the realization of *Nibāna.*"[2] His approach was informed by his recollection of childhood joy under the rose-apple tree when he was at the height of his austerities. His memory created the conditions for a compassionate approach to his predicament; it began the process by which his mother's benevolent energy was gradually returned to him. In his previous attempts to free himself, the Buddha had oscillated between his two primary strategies. In the first, under the guidance of his two well-intentioned teachers, he had sought meditative transcendence. In this approach he unconsciously mimicked that of his frightened mother, who needed to leave her body in order to tolerate her bliss. In the second, he was driven by the belief that pain and deprivation could purify him of attachment, setting his spirit free. Both strategies suffered from a split, a dualism that envisioned freedom as lying somewhere outside his everyday, ordinary experience. The Buddha's memory reoriented him, and his dreams gave him the means of knowing ordinary experience in a different way. Rather than being driven by a desire for escape, the Buddha learned to see the world as a reflection of mind. It was this capacity, evoked in him as he worked through the trauma of his mother's demise, that enabled him, in his final enlightenment, to see through death.

In the mythic retelling of the Buddha's awakening, the central narrative speaks, in symbolic form, of the Buddha's use of implicit relational knowing to see everything as a reflection of mind. In the classic version of the story, on a late-spring day not long after his five dreams, the Buddha settled himself under a fig tree close by the glistening Neranjara River and vowed not to get up until he had attained nirvana. Sitting down under the tree was no easy task, however. In the legends that have grown up over the years, it is made clear that the Buddha had to find the *exact spot* to sit upon. He was still in the process of zeroing in on his method, of finding the place of internal balance from which he could relate without strain. He tried the southern side of the tree first, but the earth began to shake as if to dissuade him. He went to the western side next, then the northern side, but the earth protested at those locations too. Finally, he settled himself on a grass seat on the eastern side of the tree. The earth was quiet there—he had found the "stable spot"[3] from which all Buddhas reach enlightenment. "My body may shrivel up, my skin, my bones, my flesh may dissolve, but I will not move from this very seat until I have obtained enlightenment," he was reputed to have declared. This stable spot was the one Ajahn Chah was referring to, the one that does not go out and bother things but sees everything as a reflection of mind.

From this spot Buddha had to face his demons. He was challenged in a series of dramatic encounters by his alter ego, Mara, a famous figure in the Buddhist world. Mara is often depicted as a devil—an embodiment of evil, death, or darkness, a kind of Buddhist version of Satan—but this is not quite right. In South Asian cosmology, Mara was actually a godlike figure, a lord of the Desire Realm, whose efforts were directed at keeping the Buddha from freeing himself from the cycle of death and rebirth. As the lord of desire, he represented the forces of clinging or craving that keep people attached to the world. Because of this, he was also intimately bound up with trauma. In psychological terms, Mara represented the Buddha's ego, "that desperate longing for a self and a world that are comprehensible, manageable, and safe."4 As ego, Mara represented the endless attempt to shield oneself from the inevitable traumas of this world. One of his nicknames was the "drought demon" because of the way he tried to hold back the waters of change. Mara was roused by the Buddha's discovery of his "stable spot." He assailed the Buddha with all kinds of trauma, trying to dislodge him from his seat of stability, much as an infant's ruthless attacks on a parent threaten her poise and self-confidence.

From the stable spot of his newly recovered implicit awareness, the Buddha was attacked by waves of Mara's forces. There are many versions of the story, depending on which sutras are consulted, but all contain three essential elements. Mara attempted to defeat Gotama with three basic strategies: "armed attack, assertion of superior merit, and attempt at seduction."5 The Buddha described this series of encounters as the deepest struggle he ever had to face: more difficult than anything he went through even at the height of his austerities. Yet he had found the perspective that enabled him to survive. Not going out to bother the forces assaulting him, he was able to see them as psychical reflections. "Only when Buddha was able to experience the desires and fears that threatened to overwhelm him as nothing but impersonal and ephemeral conditions of mind and body, did they lose their power to mesmerize him."6

In most versions of the story, the forces of aggression came first.

Mara appeared to the Buddha as a warlord mounted on an elephant commanding a legion of threatening troops.[7] He unleashed army after army, ten in all, their psychological equivalents portrayed as the following: sensual desire; discontent; hunger and thirst; craving; lethargy; fear; doubt; restlessness; longing for gain, praise, honor, and fame; and extolling oneself while disparaging others.[8] Mara hurled nine storms at the Buddha-to-be—of wind, rain, rocks, weapons, embers, ashes, sand, mud, and darkness—but the Buddha had found an "unconquerable position," an "immoveable spot"[9] from which to experience these assaults, and they rolled off him, as a child's attacks melt under the indomitable resolve and patient love of his parents. Mara's arrows of aggression turned to flowers, his rocks to garlands. The rains failed to wet Gotama; the winds failed to ruffle his composure; the embers, ashes, sand, and mud turned to blossoms and incense; and the darkness faded into Gotama's light. In later versions, developed in Mahayana Buddhism, the "immoveable spot" where Gotama sat became known as the *vajrāsana*, or "adamantine throne, in reference to its unshakable stability."[10] The relationship of this diamond seat to the mind of the mother was not only implicit: As the story continued, it became ever more clearly portrayed.

Mara's next attack was his most devious. It went straight to the heart of the Buddha's trauma and required him to reach deeply into himself to manifest what his dreams had awakened. In the most famous scene of their encounter, Mara directly challenged Gotama's sense of self-worth by asking him to prove that he was deserving of enlightenment. "By what right do you claim this seat?" he asked him. Pointing to his own armies, Mara claimed them as witnesses to his own superior standing. He was obviously an important figure, a celebrity in his own right, with legions of followers at his beck and call. "Who will be *your* witness?" Mara demanded. Gotama, who was clearly alone with no one to speak for him, appeared to have no good response. What kind of answer could he come up with when his whole approach had been based on a solitary pursuit? Having abandoned his family and friends and been forsaken by his five ascetic companions, to whom could he possibly turn to testify on his behalf? Mara's challenge was aimed directly at the most vulnerable aspect of the Buddha's psychology. If we understand Mara as the Buddha's shadow, then his question was really the Buddha's own question about himself. Deep down, the story suggests, the Buddha had unfinished business, even at the very brink of enlightenment. He was still missing something in himself, still grappling with issues of self-esteem, still trying to understand his delicate nature, still suffering from the unworthiness Mara was giving voice to.

The Buddha had another epiphany at this point. He talked about it in retrospect in language that once again evoked implicit relational knowing, as if he had remembered something long forgotten, salvaged something he did not know he had lost. There are many ways to interpret these words of the Buddha, of course, but there is no question his breakthrough involved a resurrection of forgotten feeling, a recovery of an unknown boundless presence at the heart of his aloneness. "Suppose a man wandering in a forest wilderness found an ancient path, an ancient trail, travelled by men of old, and he followed it up, and by doing so he discovered an ancient city, an ancient royal capital, where men of old had lived, with parks and groves and lakes, walled round and beautiful to see, so I too found the ancient path, the ancient trail, travelled by the Fully Enlightened Ones of old."[11]

When asked by Mara to produce a witness to his self-worth, Gotama reached out and touched the ground with his right hand. "This earth is my witness," he replied and, as if in agreement, the earth roared and shook. ("And as the Bodhisattva touched the great earth, it trembled in six ways: it trembled, trembled strongly, trembled strongly on all sides; resounded, resounded strongly, resounded strongly on all sides. Just as the bronze bells from Magadha ring out when struck with a stick, so this great earth resounded and resounded again when touched by the hand of the Bodhisattva.")[12] In many of the early representations of this famous "earth-touching gesture" (or *bhūmisparśa mudrā*), the trembling of the ground was given anthropomorphic form. The upper body of an earth goddess, named Sthāvarā or "the Stable One,"[13] emerged from the ground and bowed to Gotama with her palms together. As if the symbolism of touching the earth were not enough, the artists who later told the Buddha's story made it concrete. A mother figure appeared and affirmed her connection to the Buddha, erasing his last vestige of self-doubt, testifying to his inherent worthiness, and frightening Mara away.

In a fascinating account of the role of the earth goddess in Buddhist iconography, the scholar Miranda Shaw traced the evolution of the deity's representations in Buddhist art. She pointed out that in some versions of the story, the earth mother appeared not once but twice. In her first appearance she bore witness to the Buddha's virtue and scattered Mara and his armies. They then regrouped, and she emerged for a second time, now with a thunderous roar, threatening gestures, and a powerful quaking. Thus, two complementary aspects of the mother were embodied: In one she was a nurturing figure and in the other she displayed her aggression. In addition, Shaw pointed out how intertwined the mother and the Buddha's seat of enlightenment were. The base of the Buddha's throne intersected her womb in the first sculptures to emerge in Buddhist culture. She *was* the "stable platform"[14] of his awakening. Over later years she was portrayed as wringing rivers from her hair, washing away the forces of Mara with great cascades of water pouring down from the top of her head. She could also be seen offering the Buddha a spherical vessel in her outstretched arms, a symbol not just of fertility and abundance but also of the pregnant void of Buddhist emptiness.

Mara's third intervention involved his seductive daughters. While they were sometimes reduced to personifications of lust, his offspring were actually goddesses who Mara insisted use their "thirty-two kinds of feminine wiles"[15] to divert the Buddha from his course. But this, too, was to no avail. The almost-Buddha found that he could experience not only his aggression but also his desires as reflections his mind did not need to go out and bother. In the words of the contemporary Buddhist writer Stephen Batchelor, "this does not mean that Buddha was either unaware of these thoughts and feelings or that they no longer occurred for him. Rather than deleting them, he discovered a way of being with them in which they could gain no purchase on him."[16] The daughters of Mara, unsuccessful in their attempts to seduce the Buddha, became transformed by his presence. Just as the arrows of aggression became flowers and the rocks garlands, the forces of seduction lost their edge. The daughters returned to their father and yielded their places to eight goddesses who sang the Buddha sixteen verses of praise. Even desire could not divert the Buddha from his course.

The Buddha's enlightenment unfolded in the three watches of the night following upon his defeat of Mara. In the first watch, it is said that he remembered all of his previous existences, hundreds of thousands of them, recalling his name, race, parents, and caste, the food he ate, the length of each life, and the happiness and unhappiness he knew. The entire spectrum of his personal continuum came into view. While his awakening was also an awakening into selflessness, this did not mean that he lost the sense of his own subjective individuality. In fact, as his sense of personal trauma dissolved, as he connected with the maternal energy his implicit memory had unknowingly kept him apart from, his own existence across time became clear. The present became thick with the past and his sense of "stretching along between past and future,"[17] the "unifying thread of temporality,"[18] returned. While the traditional accounts are redolent with his recovery of past lives, in psychological terms the recovery of the first watch of the night speaks of the Buddha's recognition of just that sense of subjective knowing that I was attempting to communicate to my father on his deathbed. From the stable spot of self-observation under the Bodhi Tree, with the earth mother as his witness, the Buddha was able to see things as they were. First and foremost, this involved seeing the vast horizon of his personal subjectivity. His individual flow of personhood revealed itself without obstruction.

In the second watch of the night, the Buddha understood what the therapist Robert Stolorow has called "the unbearable embeddedness of being."[19] He viscerally grasped the "inescapable contingency" of everyday life and began to formulate his theory of karma to explain it. "Moved by compassion," one of his biographers has written, the Buddha "opened his wisdom eye further and saw the spectacle of the whole universe as in a spotless mirror. He saw beings being born and passing away in accordance with karma, the laws of cause and effect."[20] This vision, held in the compassionate embrace of his mindful awareness, helped guide the Buddha toward his final goal. Attuned to all of the unbearable affect of the relational world, he had no need for any kind of defensive fortifications in the face of it. As Stephen Batchelor has written, "When the stubborn, frozen solidity of necessary selves and things is dissolved in the perspective of emptiness, a contingent world opens up that is fluid and ambiguous, fascinating and terrifying. Not only does this world unfold before us with awesome subtlety, complexity, and majesty, one day it will swallow us up in its tumultuous wake along with everything else we cherish. The infinitely poignant beauty of creation is inseparable from its diabolic destructiveness. How to live in such a turbulent world with wisdom, tolerance, empathy, care, and nonviolence is what saints and philosophers have struggled over the centuries to articulate. What is striking about the Buddhist approach is that rather than positing an immortal or transcendent self that is immune to the vicissitudes of the world, Buddha insisted that salvation lies in discarding such consoling fantasies and embracing instead the very stuff of life that will destroy you."[21]

Batchelor's description of the Buddha's opening brings to mind a reaction to my cell-phone meditation that I heard about secondhand. One of my friends told me that after hearing me lead the meditation she went home and told her husband about it. Her spouse, a highly accomplished but troubled man who had struggled deeply with addiction for much of his adult life, burst into tears when she described it to him. She was surprised by his uncharacteristic response—it was not his habit to burst into tears. He was withdrawn from her and had become increasingly isolated and unemotional. When she asked him why he was crying, he said that the idea of letting life in, listening to it and accepting it was so much the opposite of how he was living that he was overwhelmed. The amount of pain he imagined in the room both moved and unnerved him.

His response, while extreme, highlights the radical nature of the Buddha's approach. As he said immediately after his awakening, it really does go against the stream. In our efforts to manage our own traumas, in our attempts to suppress them or make them go away, we close ourselves off like my friend's husband had. We shy away from our own pain and we certainly shy away from the pain of others. We feel filled up already and afraid of being further contaminated. And we are so busy managing our own stress that we forget the humanity—the compassion—that brought my friend's husband to tears.

The paradoxical nature of the Buddhist stance is evident in the traditional descriptions of his awakening. On the one hand, dissolving the stubborn solidity of self and other opens up a flow—and a compassionate awareness—that can outlast destruction, much as the mother's survival of her infant's rage does. On the other hand, the surrender of the self into implicit relational knowing also reveals the impermanence that will eventually consume one. It was this paradox that the Buddha's final insights resolved. In the realizations that dawned, he came to fully appreciate the inexhaustible body of bliss that had so frightened his mother at the time of his birth.

In the third watch of the night, the Buddha understood what he later articulated as the Four Noble Truths: suffering, its cause, the bliss of its cessation, and the path to its relief. He stared straight into the fire, saw that everything was burning, and, in the process, felt the flames of craving blowing out. In no longer resisting the imperfections of life, he saw it transform. Nirvana dawned just as the morning star first appeared. "Done is what had to be done," the Buddha declared. And then he uttered his famous statement about the eradication of ignorance, "Oh, housebuilder! You have now been seen. You shall build the house no longer." Later on, when describing his new understanding, the Buddha phrased it something like like this: "What other people call happiness, I call suffering. What other people call suffering, I call happiness." With the fire of craving blown out, the Buddha realized what has come to be called the wisdom that goes beyond wisdom. In keeping with the metaphor of intrinsic relational knowing essential to the psychology of the Buddha, the Tibetan name for his metawisdom (*Mahāmudrā*) translates as "the Great Embrace." The knowledge that goes beyond knowledge is relational. In the third watch of the night, the Buddha saw clearly that we all have within us the means of dealing with trauma. As one important sutra has put it, "If we are not hampered by our confused subjectivity, this our worldly life is an activity of Nirvana itself."[22]

Fifteen hundred years after the life of the Buddha, his teachings moved to Tibet. One of the Indian Buddhists who brought those teachings there was a Bengali monk named Atisha, born in 980 CE, who was one of the most accomplished masters of his time. Once asked by his Tibetan followers to summarize the Buddha's realizations, Atisha gave a famous response. It is denser and more comprehensive than what I was able to say to my father, but at its heart was the same implicit relational knowing that became the Buddha's diamond throne. Its combination of wisdom and kindness defines the Middle Path.

"The highest skill lies in the realization of selflessness," said Atisha. "The highest nobility lies in taming your own mind. The highest excellence lies in having the attitude that seeks to help others. The highest precept is continual mindfulness. The highest remedy lies in understanding the intrinsic transcendence of everything. The highest activity lies in not conforming with worldly concerns. The highest mystic realization lies in lessening and transmuting the passions. The highest charity lies in nonattachment. The highest morality lies in having a peaceful mind. The highest tolerance lies in humility. The highest effort lies in abandoning attachment to works. The highest meditation lies in the mind without claims. The highest wisdom lies in not grasping anything as being what it appears to be."

Still looking for something more, his followers had one additional question. "And what is the ultimate goal of the teaching?" they asked.

"The ultimate goal of the teaching is that emptiness whose essence is compassion,"[23] he responded. Even though we can't find what is knowing, he might have said, knowing is there.

In bringing implicit relational knowing out of his unconscious, the Buddha healed the rupture of the beginning of his life. Having solved his own problem, he did not disappear. His own trauma alerted him to the traumas of others. For the rest of his life, until his own death from food poisoning forty-five years later, he shared his understanding freely. Aligned with that emptiness whose essence is compassion, he showed others how to be mindful of their own minds. Resting in awareness, seeing the world as a mirror, he helped people know trauma, not only as trauma but as a bearable, if inevitable, consequence of an unstable world. Experienced as a reflection of mind, even trauma could be enlightening.

12

A Relational Home

Clear-eyed, compassionate, and awake, the Buddha was a realist. With no dust obscuring his vision, he was able to sum up the entire human predicament in a single word. "*Dukkha!*" he exclaimed in his First Noble Truth as he held to his vow to speak the beneficial truth even if it was disagreeable. Suffering! Its reality permeates our lives, shadowing the good times and insinuating itself into everything. Trauma is a basic fact of life, according to the Buddha. It is not just an occasional thing that happens only to some people; it is there all the time. Things are always slipping away. Although there are occasions when it is more pronounced and awful and occasions when it is actually horrific, trauma does not just happen to a few unlucky people. It is the bedrock of our biology. Churning, chaotic, and unpredictable, our lives are stretched across a tenuous canvas. Much of our energy goes into resisting this fragility, yet it is there nonetheless. The Buddha found it useful to put people in touch with their vulnerability, yet he had one important qualification to his dictum to always speak the constructive but distasteful truth. Only if he knew the time to say it would he confront people with their traumas. Only if the relationship could sustain it would he gentle them into themselves. In specifying this, the Buddha was making an important point, one not lost on today's psychotherapists. Trauma becomes sufferable, even illuminating, when there is a relational home[1] to hold it in. Without this, it is simply too much to bear.

The Buddha did not come to this understanding out of nowhere. His own personal journey involved coming to terms with the loss of a mother he, for all intents and purposes, never knew. As therapists who specialize in "developmental" or "relational" trauma have come to realize, the first few years of life are critical for one's self-esteem and self-confidence. The healthy attachment of a baby to a "good-enough" parent facilitates a comfort with emotional experience that makes the challenges of adult life and adult intimacy less intimidating. When there is serious malattunement in early life, however, there is often a traumatic residue that manifests in surprising and disturbing ways. The Buddha, like many of us, acted out this residue. Abandoning his wife and child, debasing himself in the forest striving to liberate himself from his mind and body, his spiritual journey can be read, from one perspective at least, as an expression of primitive agony.

Primitive agonies exist in many of us. Originating in painful experiences that occurred before we had the cognitive capacities to know what was happening, they tend to blindside us, traumatizing us again and again as we find ourselves enacting a pain we do not understand. The Buddha's story is a perfect motif for this. At the heart of his life was a trauma he would not have been able to remember: the loss of the mother who so delighted in him for the first week of his life. This loss lay hidden in his implicit memory, coloring his experience in ways he could feel but never know, encouraging a feeling of self-hatred and discontent. As one of today's leading neuroscientists, Joseph LeDoux, has put it after studying the impact of stress on the brain, emotional memory may be forever.[2] The Buddha, his emotional memory imprinted with profound loss, had to work with one of the most fundamental traumas of everyday life: the death of a loved one. And he had to do it by himself, without the interpersonal support he always gave to others.

The Buddha made it clear that the way out of suffering is by going through it. He taught the Four Noble Truths and the Four Foundations of Mindfulness as the means of doing just this. Beginning with the breath, expanding to the body, feelings, states of mind, and awareness itself, the progression of mindfulness teaches that trauma can be used to open the mind. When we are no longer dissociating critical aspects of our experience, setting ourselves up in opposition to elements we are trying to avoid, we can finally relax. The Buddha had a taste of this when he remembered his childhood joy under the rose-apple tree. Settling into himself without falling prey to his usual set of self-judgments, he had his first sense of the collaborative communication his mind was capable of. He became a vessel for feelings, reproducing the delight his mother had felt herself unable to contain, while also touching the fear that came to consume both mother and child. In the reconfiguration of his method that followed, the Buddha found that feelings did not have to frighten him. Even the unpleasant ones of primitive agony could be attended to with sufficient practice. Trauma could be known, not only as a personal tragedy but as an impersonal reflection of an underlying and universal reality. Suffering is part and parcel of human existence. It is in all of us, in one form or another. The choice we have is how to relate to it. We can try to avoid it or we can use it as grist for the mill.

Western therapists have long recognized how urgently the self wishes to keep trauma from disturbing the peace. As Winnicott's biographer, Adam Phillips, has written, "The ego in the Freudian story—ourselves as we prefer to be seen—is like a picture with a frame around it, and the function of the frame is to keep the picture intact."[3] That which is unacceptable to the self—the traumatic residue, for instance—

is denied or extruded. Anything that might cause too much anxiety is taken out of the picture. In the Western view, the best one can hope for is an oscillation between honest self-examination and dissociation. "Only the dialectic, the see-saw, between recognition and misrecognition makes things bearable; were we to straightforwardly recognize the essential aspects of ourselves, it is suggested, we would not be able to bear the anxiety."[4]

The Buddha saw another possibility. Slowly but surely, he found, it is possible to expand the frame. Beginning with the breath and gradually learning to include the entire panoply of human experience, it is possible to develop mindfulness to degrees not envisioned by most Western therapists. The key, taught the Buddha, lies in not taking trauma personally. When it is seen as a natural reflection of the chaotic universe of which we are a part, it loses its edge and can become a deeper object of mindfulness. In the famous stories of Kisagotami and Paṭācārā, victims of what we would call unspeakable traumas, this was the Buddha's first intervention. "You thought that you alone had lost a son. The law of death is that among all living creatures there is no permanence," he told Kisagotami. "It is not only today that you have met with calamity and disaster," he cautioned Paṭācārā, "but throughout this beginningless round of existence, weeping over the loss of sons and others dear to you, you have shed more tears than the waters of the four oceans." You think the suffering is *your* suffering, taught the Buddha, but all suffering is one. This does not mean that it stops being painful, but, like the splinter in his foot, it becomes an inevitable consequence of a human embodiment.

Not all traumas are inevitable consequences of human embodiments, however. Many of them involve willful choices made by conscious human beings to inflict pain on others. It is not the most helpful thing to say to a victim of torture or sexual abuse that their trauma is nothing personal. Yet the Buddha's teachings offer something important in these cases too. A patient of mine put it very succinctly. After many years in therapy, he began to talk once again about times he was molested in his youth. He had told me the details when he first came into therapy but had not talked about it much since. "I've talked about the *events*," he said, "but never about my feelings about them." As the Buddha articulated, feelings matter. They are the bridge between the personal and whatever lies beyond. When my patient was able to talk about the profound disappointment he felt in the people he had most trusted, he was able to relate to his own experience much more compassionately. In the place of his chronic shame and self-criticism came a mourning and sadness for the boy he had once been. He began to see how one consequence of his abuse was the way he was keeping people who legitimately cared about him at bay. When feelings like my patient's are not acknowledged, a protective cover is required. The frame of our ego boxes us in and our lives are foreshortened. We remain tied to the past, fearing something that has already happened but that we have never fully known.

Therapists of war veterans returning from Iraq and Afghanistan have found something similar. A particularly astute therapist, Dr. Russell Carr, has written about his work with these veterans in a way that parallels my patient's insight. Inspired by Stolorow's *Trauma and Human Existence* and using one particular soldier's experience as a case study, Dr. Carr spelled out the path of recovery. "It is not the violence he witnessed in Afghanistan that haunts him; it is his feelings about the violence *he* inflicted. He often maintained that, given the circumstances again, he would kill the same people, but that doesn't make it any more bearable."[5] Dr. Carr's veteran needed a relational home for his feelings of guilt and anguish. Before working with his therapist, he had no such home and no way to make sense of his feelings, let alone admit to them. His only notion was that, as a soldier, he should be able to handle anything. The frame of his ego required that he be solid as a rock. Unable to be so, he drank. Dissociating from the troubling feelings, he remained haunted by them. Stuck in his implicit memory, they never could be acknowledged. He needed to talk with another person so that he could make some sense of things. Only then could he let down his guard and feel like a person again. As Dr. Carr put it, "In the absence of a sustaining relational home where feelings can be verbalized, understood, and held, emotional pain can become a source of unbearable shame and self-loathing."[6]

Carr's finding that the trauma lay not in the violence his patient witnessed but in the "feelings about the violence *he* inflicted" is instructive. Unbearable feelings become tolerable when the capacity for mindful knowing is strengthened. We don't have to be war veterans to experience unbearable anguish, although this does not diminish the horror of what war veterans have gone through. But as the Buddha made clear, we all have to deal with something. Trauma is a fact of everyday life. Just staying with the issue of anger: We all have shame and anguish about the violence *we* have inflicted. Wishing that it were not so does not make it go away.

But we do wish. A patient came in to my office recently and asked me for a favor. He wanted to know if I could give his wife a mantra to help her manage her pain and stress. She was used to working very hard but was getting older and was being nudged, ever so surely, out of her privileged position at work. She didn't know what to do with herself and was becoming increasingly anxious. She knew that her husband was getting something out of working with me and hoped I could work some magic for her. I wished I had a mantra for her. But I recognized this as another example of someone resisting the trauma of everyday life. If only there was a formula that could make it disappear! I told my patient that one of the traditional functions of mantra in the East was to open a space of longing. Imploring God, through the repetition of his name, to help us accept the traumas that have befallen us and take responsibility for those we have caused, is very different from asking Him to restore us to perfect harmony. My patient's wife did not believe in God, but he thought she would grasp the point. Trying to blot out trauma leaves us vulnerable to enacting its residue. He thought she might be able to devise her own mantra, one that made room for imperfection and disappointment but also connected her to the tenderness he knew she harbored.

The Buddha's most fundamental discovery was that the human mind is, in itself, the relational home that is needed to process trauma. While we all tend to think of ourselves as isolated individuals adrift in a hostile universe, the Buddha ultimately saw this way of thinking as delusional. It may feel as if you are all alone, he taught, but that is not the whole picture. We are relational creatures, our minds reflecting the organizational patterns of our earliest interactions. If you go into aloneness without the customary fear, you may be surprised at the sense of unknown boundless presence you will find. The implicit relational knowing of the mother is hardwired into each of our minds. Obscured by our habits of thought, by our egocentric self-preoccupations, and by the primitive agonies that hold us in their grip, this illimitable awareness is already there for the asking. It is a renewable resource, ever present, accessible to those willing to go through the traumas of everyday life to find it. Good therapists make this palpable in the interpersonal environment. They replicate the holding environment of Winnicott's mother–infant dynamic and create a context in which difficult feelings can be known as they never could before. But the Buddha's insight took this one important step further.

The Buddha's story illustrates that a relational home can ultimately be found within. This does not mean there is no place for psychotherapy, no role for therapists like Winnicott or Carr, only that the function of such interventions will ultimately be to point the way toward this truth. In losing his mother at such an early age, the Buddha affirmed the underlying and inescapable anguish at the heart of existence. While it is compelling to read his journey toward enlightenment as a process of coming to terms with this trauma, I believe it is much more. Not only did he find a way of awakening to and releasing his own pain, he figured out something that applies across the board. As the Buddha made clear, suffering is a universal truth. While the things that bother us cannot always be eliminated, we can change the way we relate to them. In uncovering the inherent relational capacity of the mind, which finds its natural expression in a mother's concern for her baby, he found the transformative medicine he was looking for. Trauma, if it doesn't destroy us, wakes us up both to our own relational capacities and to the suffering of others. Not only does it make us hurt, it makes us more human, caring, and wise.

There is a beautiful example of this in the annals of Tibetan Buddhism. An eighteenth-century Mongolian monk, Jankya Rolway Dorje, wrote a poem in the immediate aftermath of his awakening that spoke of his personal agony while clearly laying out the role of trauma in waking up the mind. In so doing, he even anticipated the fundamental rule of Freudian psychoanalysis. "I will speak spontaneously whatever comes to mind!" he began, sounding for all the world like a patient on an analytic couch. He was, in a real sense, writing his own mantra. "I was like a mad child, long lost his old mother. Never could find her, though she was with him always!" Rolway Dorje's poem literally equated the smiling face of the mother with the implicit relational knowing of the enlightened mind. In his day-to-day reality, as he explained in his verse, he was struggling with feelings of abandonment. While he was already an accomplished lama with a bevy of intellectual and spiritual attainments, in his heart of hearts he was still a crazed and lonely child. No longer pretending otherwise, Rolway Dorje was able, as a prelude to his awakening, to acknowledge and articulate his personal version of *dukkha*. His trauma was no longer dissociated, no longer stuck in his implicit memory; it was available to his conscious mind and able to be used as an object of mindfulness. Dropping the more accomplished and self-protective aspects of his identity, expanding the frame of his ego, he stopped pushing away the mad feelings he was most ashamed of. Able to experience himself without the usual filters of self-judgment, Rolway Dorje had a breakthrough. The mother he was seeking in concrete physical form showed herself within. "But now it seems I'm about to find that kind old Mother," his poem continued, "Since relationality hints where she hides. I think, 'Yes, yes!'—then 'No, no!'—then, 'Could it be, really!' These various subjects and objects are my Mother's smiling face! These births, deaths, and changes are my Mother's lying words! My undeceiving Mother has deceived me!"[7] His own relational awareness, the very essence of the mother he was seeking, came to the fore. The home he was in search of was already present within. Knowing was there, and it was with him always.

Rolway Dorje's verse was called "The Song of the View." This title referred back to the Buddha's Eightfold Path, to his menu for awakening, which consisted of Realistic View, Motivation, Speech, Action, Livelihood, Effort, Mindfulness, and Concentration. The Buddha explained it for the first time in his teaching on the Four Noble Truths. The Eightfold Path was the Fourth Noble Truth: the way out of suffering. One of the interesting things about the Eightfold Path is the importance the Buddha gave to Realistic View. It came first. Meditation, in the form of Mindfulness and Concentration, came last. Realistic View was concerned with the attitude one takes toward one's existence and one's suffering: toward the traumas of everyday life. Before meditation could be of much use, the Eightfold Path made clear, one had to educate the thinking mind. Realistic View was the means of explaining how people could reorient themselves. When that happened successfully, as the Mongolian lama's poem described, real transformation was possible.

The usual inclination, the one Rolway Dorje quite probably was subject to prior to his breakthrough, was to hunt for some kind of "absolute" escape from the world of suffering. In the spiritual traditions of South Asia, long present before the time of the Buddha, this vision of escape was well established. The Buddha was subject to it too, as his attempts to wipe suffering away during his time in the forest made clear. The Buddha was radical, even in his own time, for eventually proposing another approach. While it may not have been such a revelatory proclamation to say that suffering was an inescapable fact of life, the conclusion the Buddha came to ran counter to most people's desires.

The most important thing we can do about suffering is to acknowledge it. Simply acknowledging it, while seeming like a minor adjustment, is actually huge. A friend of mine told me how, when his mother died when he was five years old, his father told him one morning that she was gone and would not be coming back and then never talked about her again. While extreme, this response is emblematic of our natural instincts. We would like to pretend that everything is okay, that death does not touch us, that we are not possessed by primitive agonies whose origins are murky at best, that we are somehow immune from the unbearable embeddedness of existance. But trauma is part of our definition as human beings. It is inextricably woven into the fabric of our lives. No one can escape it. Acknowledging it, as Realistic View encourages us to do, brings us closer to the incomprehensible reality of our own deaths. And as far as death is concerned, the way out is most definitely through.

As a therapist, I have found this approach to be enormously helpful, even for people with no relationship to Buddhism and no interest in meditation. If it is a truth, I long ago decided, it must be true no matter what religion one does or does not believe in. Many people, in the aftermath of an acute trauma like the loss of a loved one, for instance, believe they should be able to "get over it" within a discrete period of time. There are five stages of grief, they remind me, quoting the Swiss psychiatrist Elisabeth Kübler-Ross: denial, anger, bargaining, depression, and acceptance. They should be able to go through them in a year or two, they believe. I am cautious in my response. The Buddha took a different approach, one that seems more realistic. There need be no end to grief, he would say. While it is never static—it is not a single (or even a five-stage) thing—there is no reason to believe it will disappear for good and no need to judge oneself if it does not. Grief turns over and over. It is vibrant, surprising and alive, just as we are.

In a similar way, the primitive agonies of our childhoods live on into adulthood. Many of my patients, conditioned by Western psychology, feel that once they have some understanding of where their feelings come from, they should be finished with them. But we are not built that way. Primitive feelings continue to be stirred up throughout adult life. Understanding them does not turn them off. They are our history, our emotional memories; part of the people we have become. A patient of mine whose mother killed herself when my patient was four years old became unusually anxious when she was engaged to be married recently. She knew why, of course. What if her new husband were to disappear as precipitously as her mother did? But knowing why was not what the Buddha meant by Realistic View. He meant something much more direct. Realistic View means examining feelings rather than running away from them, acknowledging trauma rather than pretending all is normal. My patient's betrothal gave her another chance to face emotions that had been too overwhelming to face at the time of her mother's death. She was being given a window into herself, into her history and into her pain. In taking possession of those traumatic feelings, she was also being freed from the grip of them. Rather than enacting her panic and fleeing from her new husband, she could settle in to her present-day relationship with a newfound compassion for the bereft girl still soldiering on inside herself. Like a mad child long lost her old mother, my patient came to see that the maternal energy she needed was actually present within. Changing her attitude, changing the way she related to her panicky feelings, gave her access to that all-important energy and allowed her to go forward in her life.

In the Zen tradition of China, the wisdom of the Buddha's awakening has been preserved in a collection of one hundred koans called the Blue Cliff Record. These koans, dating from the eleventh-century Sung Dynasty, dare students to move beyond their conventional ways of thinking and to align their minds with the perfection of wisdom implicit in their true natures. They pose paradoxical questions that are meant to confuse the thinking mind and open access to an alternative channel of communication. Working with them is a means of cultivating Realistic View. The koans challenge the mind just as trauma does, asking us to make sense of the inconceivable and to explain the unexplainable. Many of the koans play on the notion of suffering and its release, pointing the way toward the Buddha's own transformative vision. The memory of his childhood joy under the rose-apple tree can be seen as an early example of a koan. It confounded the Buddha at first but eventually transformed the way he oriented himself in the world.

The koans in the Blue Cliff Record do their best to introduce people to their true natures. One of them (number 27 out of 100) quotes a monk asking the master Yun Men, "How is it when the tree withers and the leaves fall?" There are many ways to interpret the question, of course. On one level, it is an allusion to old age, death or the loss of a loved one. The tree withers and the leaves fall just as the body shrivels and the life runs out. On another level, the koan speaks of the more fundamental question of trauma. What is it like when our defenses wither, when we stop believing in the absolutisms of everyday life? What happens when we surrender the reassuring myths we use to prop ourselves up, when the stable and predictable world is revealed as fluid, chaotic, and tumultuous, when the isolated self recognizes its own embeddedness of being? Therapists who study trauma know what happens in such cases. As Stolorow has written, a "deep chasm" opens "in which an anguished sense of estrangement and solitude takes form."[8] Yet the Blue Cliff Record, fueled by the Buddha's discoveries, comes to a different conclusion.

The classical answer, the one given by Yun Men, a master so irascible that he forbade his disciples to record any of his notoriously abstruse sayings (forcing them to surreptitiously write them down on a paper robe) was: "Body exposed in the golden wind."[9] Even before I tried to grapple with what Yun Men was saying, I loved his response. Something about it made me happy, this body exposed in a golden wind. I imagined myself on a beach, the sun-drenched air gusting off the water, feeling safe, warm, and connected even while I lay there alone. With the leaves falling, without the usual array of comforts and consolations, in the depths of my solitude, was an unknown boundless presence: a golden wind enveloping my uncovered form.

The question asked of Yun Men, "How is it when the tree withers and the leaves fall?" also refers back to all of the trees that were so important in the life history of the Buddha, trees that offered him shelter and support as he confronted the world of suffering. His mother grasped the low-hanging limb of a *sala* tree as she gave birth to him from her side. He sat under the shade of a rose-apple tree as a youth and felt an inexplicable joy arise in the midst of his aloneness, the memory of which reoriented him on his path to enlightenment. And he found the exact spot for his awakening under a fig tree by the sparkling Neranjara River; a tree, now known as the *bodhi tree*, a descendant of which still flourishes on that spot in the North Indian village of Bodh Gaya. The koan asks us to imagine what it would be like if even those trees were to wither and die. It refers back to the death of the Buddha's mother, for whom the trees, in his biography, serve as a kind of stand-in. And the answer, in the form of the golden wind, comes through loud and clear. The Buddha's relational home was not dependent on any external thing: not on any of the trees and not even on the continuing presence of his biological mother. Even when he was completely exposed, it was there with him. As important as the trees may have been as placeholders along the way, his liberation came, purely and simply, from within.

In Yun Men's time, there was a famous saying that attempted to capture this important truth. Buddha, the saying inferred, was able to open himself "fearlessly and calmly to the tumult of the sublime."[10] "The Buddhas of past, present, and future turn the Great Wheel of Dharma upon flames of fire," this saying read, making reference to the Buddha's Fire Sermon, to his well-known teaching that everything is burning. Yun Men turned even this version around.

"The flames of fire expound the Dharma," he is reputed to have said. "The Buddhas of past, present, and future stand there and listen."[11]

The koan of the tree withering and its leaves falling also unwittingly ties into the work of Winnicott on developmental trauma. When he was sixty-seven years old, Winnicott, uncharacteristically, wrote a very personal poem about his own mother. The poem, which is called "The Tree," seemed to have emerged rather unexpectedly. It conjured up the favorite tree in his family's garden that Winnicott climbed to do his homework in when he was a boy. Winnicott sent the poem to his brother-in-law with the following note: "Do you mind seeing this that hurt coming out of me. I think it had some thorns sticking out somehow. It's not happened to me before & I hope it doesn't again."

The key lines of the poem are the following:

Mother below is weeping
weeping
weeping
Thus I knew her
Once, stretched out on her lap
as now on dead tree
I learned to make her smile
to stem her tears
to undo her guilt
to cure her inward death
To enliven her was my living.[12]

Knowing Winnicott's work, one can read all kinds of things into the poem, including the fact that his mother's maiden name was Woods. But even without knowing much about his work, the basic theme is evident. His mother's smiling face did not make itself spontaneously available to him—young Donald had to work for it. To Winnicott's way of thinking, this was a form of trauma. A child whose mother was either intrusive or abandoning has to prematurely mobilize a self in order to manage the less than adequate parental environment. This prematurely mobilized self is a life-saving adaptation that eventually squeezes out life. It comes at the expense of the kind of play a more secure child can engage in and results in a self whose rigidity and inflexibility ultimately creates fear or deadness. As a vehicle for connecting with the much beloved parent, such a "caretaker self" has extra staying power, extra value, and extra investment. It is etched deeply into the brain; wired, through a combination of love and necessity, into the fabric of one's personality. But as a vehicle for connecting more deeply with life, the caretaker self is flawed. Based on an insecure attachment, its stance is inherently mistrustful.

"To enliven her was my living," Winnicott wrote, with a play on the word "living." It was his job, and it was also his life: All that he could focus on. This was the classic scenario for Winnicott, the one he described over and over again, in which something critical in the child is sacrificed in order to cope with a less than adequate emotional environment. Winnicott was writing his own version of the koan here. He was describing the trauma that happens when the tree (or mother) withers and her leaves fall. But Winnicott was also demonstrating, in a very personal way, what the Buddha found. The way out of trauma is by going through it. In acknowledging, without rancor, the deadness of his maternal environment, Winnicott was able to turn himself into the relational home he had lacked. He did this for countless patients and he did it for himself.

The golden wind refers back to the implicit relational knowing of the mother, latent in all of us. When our traumas are exposed, when the efforts to resist, deny, overcome or even indulge them are dropped, something unexpected happens. Connection analogous to that of the infant-mother couple naturally arises. A golden wind appears. While it frightened the Buddha when he first remembered it blowing through him under the rose-apple tree, he was curious enough to explore it unabashedly from that moment on. Eventually he found it to be a breeze.

Acknowledgments

To Robert Thurman for showing me the meaning of words; to Sharon Salzberg, Joseph Goldstein, and Jack Kornfield for giving me the opportunity to teach with them; to Dan Harris for meaningful conversation; to Ann Epstein for implicit relational knowing and Bernard Edelstein and Michael Vincent Miller for Bromberg; to Mike Eigen for feeling mattering; Nancy Black for Stolorow and Lisa Gornick for the baby's first steps. To Amy Gross, Robby Stein, Axel Hoffer, and Lindsay Whalen for their careful readings of the text. To Henk Barendregt for Rilke and the "courage de luxe." To Ann Godoff for guiding me and Anne Edelstein for caring for the book. To Sonia for help with the brain, Will for his support, and Arlene for her understanding.

Notes

Chapter One: The Way Out Is Through

1. Robert Stolorow, *Trauma and Human Existence: Autobiographical, Psychoanalytic, and Philosophical Reflections* (New York: Routledge, 2007), p. 10.
2. *The Dhammapada.* Copyright, P. Lal, Writer's Workshop, 162/92 Lake Gardens, Calcutta, India 7004S (New York: Farrar, Straus & Giroux, 1967), p. 115.
3. Walpola Rahula, *What the Buddha Taught* (New York: Grove, 1974), p. 22.
4. Richard Gombrich, *What the Buddha Thought* (London: Equinox, 2009), p. 161.
5. *Ibid.*
6. Joseph Goldstein, *Abiding in Mindfulness*, vol. 1, Sounds True. See also Analayo Satipatthāna, *The Direct Path to Realization* (Cambridge, Windhorse, 2003), p. 244
7. Richard Gombrich, *What the Buddha Thought* (London: Equinox, 2009), p. 166.
8. As recounted in *George, Being George: George Plimpton's Life as Told, Admired, Deplored and Envied by 200 Friends, Lovers, Aquaintances, Rivals—and a Few Unappreciative Observers.* Edited by Nelson W. Aldrich, Jr. (New York: Random House, 2008), p. 89.
9. Sharon Salzberg first made me aware of this apparent contradiction.

Chapter Two: Primitive Agony

1. Bhikkhu Ñāṇamoli, *The Life of the Buddha: According to the Pali Canon* (Kandy, Sri Lanka: Buddhist Publication Society, 1972/1992), pp. 32, 38.
2. *Ibid.*, p. 39.
3. *Ibid.*, p. 40.
4. Walpola Rahula, *What the Buddha Taught* (New York: Grove, 1974), p. 12.
5. Bhikkhu Ñāṇamoli and Bhikkhu Bodhi, trans., *The Middle Length Discourses of the Buddha: A New Translation of the Majjhima Nikāya* (Boston: Wisdom, 1995), MN ii, 258, p. 865.
6. D. W. Winnicott, "The Theory of the Parent-Infant Relationship," in *The Motivational Processes and the Facilitating Environment* (New York: International Universities Press, 1965), p. 39, no 1.
7. Sandra Boynton, *What's Wrong, Little Pookie?* (New York: Random House, 2007).
8. Robert Stolorow, *Trauma and Human Existence: Autobiographical, Psychoanalytic, and Philosophical Reflections* (New York: Routledge, 2007), pp. 3–4.
9. *Ibid.*, p. 1.

10. Deborah Baker, *A Blue Hand: The Beats in India* (New York: Penguin, 2008), pp. 202–3.
11. Nyanaponika Thera, *The Heart of Buddhist Meditation* (New York: Samuel Weiser, 1962), p. 30.
12. D. W. Winnicott, *Babies and Their Mothers* (Reading, MA: Addison-Wesley, 1988), pp. 36–38.
13. Krishna Das, *Chants of a Lifetime* (Carlsbad, CA: Hay House, 2010), p. 172.

Chapter Three: Everything Is Burning

1. Richard Gombrich, *What the Buddha Thought* (London: Equinox, 2009), p. 113.
2. *Ibid.*, p. 111.
3. Bhikkhu Ñāṇamoli, *The Life of the Buddha: According to the Pali Canon* (Kandy, Sri Lanka: Buddhist Publication Society, 1972/1992), p. 64.
4. Gombrich, *What the Buddha Thought*, p. 112.
5. *Ibid.*
6. *Ibid.*
7. *Ibid.*, p. 113.
8. *Ibid.*, p. 33.
9. Robert Stolorow, *Trauma and Human Existence: Autobiographical, Psychoanalytic, and Philosophical Reflections* (New York: Routledge, 2007), p. 10.
10. Gombrich, *What the Buddha Thought*, p. 20.
11. Lucien Stryk, *World of the Buddha* (New York: Grove Weidenfeld, 1968), pp. 173–74.
12. *Ibid.*, p. 174.
13. D. W. Winnicott, *Playing and Reality* (London and New York: Routledge, 1971), p. 11.
14. Michael Eigen, *Contact with the Depths* (London: Karnac, 2011), p. 13.

Chapter Four: The Rush to Normal

1. Sherab Chödzin Kohn, *A Life of the Buddha* (Boston: Shambhala, 2009), p. 7.
2. *Ibid.*
3. Bhikkhu Ñāṇamoli, *The Life of the Buddha: According to the Pali Canon* (Kandy, Sri Lanka: Buddhist Publication Society, 1972/1992), p. 8.
4. *Ibid.*, pp. 8–9.
5. Robert Stolorow, *Trauma and Human Existence: Autobiographical, Psychoanalytic, and Philosophical Reflections* (New York: Routledge, 2007), p. 16.
6. *Ibid.*
7. *Ibid.*
8. *Ibid.*
9. Nyanaponika Thera and Hellmuth Hecker, *Great Disciples of the Buddha* (Boston: Wisdom, 2003), pp. 293–300.
10. *Ibid.*, p. 295.
11. *Ibid.*
12. *Ibid.* p. 297.
13. *Ibid.*, p. 300.
14. Michael Eigen, *The Electrified Tightrope* (London: Karnac, 1993/2004), p. 133.
15. Stolorow, *Trauma and Human Existence*, p. 16.

Chapter Five: Dissociation

1. Jon Kabat-Zinn, *Full Catastrophe Living: Using the Wisdom of Your Body and Mind to Face Stress, Pain, and Illness* (New York: Delacorte, 1990).
2. Philip M. Bromberg, *Standing in the Spaces* (Hillsdale, NJ: Analytic Press, 1998), p. 190.

3. *The Voice of the Buddha: The Beauty of Compassion, Volume I*, translated by Gwendolyn Bays (Berkeley, CA: Dharma, 1983), p. 147.

4. Miranda Shaw, *Buddhist Goddesses of India* (Princeton, NJ: Princeton University Press, 2006), p. 46.

5. Anahad O'Connor, "Obituary: Nicholas Hughes, 47, Sylvia Plath's Son," *New York Times*, March 21, 2009.

6. Ashva·ghosha, *Life of the Buddha*, trans. Patrick Olivelle (New York: New York University Press, 2008), p. 73.

7. Bromberg, *Standing in the Spaces*, p. 6.

8. Philip M. Bromberg, *Awakening the Dreamer* (Mahwah, NJ: Analytic Press, 2006), p. 33.

9. *Ibid.*

10. *Ibid.*, p. 7.

11. Ashva·ghosha, *Life of the Buddha*, p. 41.

12. D. W. Winnicott, "Primitive Emotional Development" (1945), in *Collected Papers: Through Paediatrics to Psycho-Analysis* (New York: Basic Books, 1958), p. 154.

13. Ashva·ghosha, *Life of the Buddha*, p. 11.

14. D. W. Winnicott, *"The Newborn and His Mother"* (1964), in *Babies and Their Mothers* (Reading, MA: Addison-Wesley, 1988), pp. 30–31.

15. D. W. Winnicott, "Postscript: D.W.W. on D.W.W." (1967), in *Psychoanalytic Explorations* (Cambridge, MA: Harvard University Press, 1989), p. 580.

16. *Ibid.*

17. *The Minor Anthologies of the Pali Canon: Part II, Verses of Uplift (Udana)*, translated by F. L. Woodward (London: Pali Text Society, 1948), p. 57.

Chapter Six: Curiosity

1. Michael Eigen, *Eigen in Seoul: Volume One: Madness and Murder* (London: Karnac, 2010), p. 5.

2. *Ibid.*

3. *Ibid.*, p. 9.

Chapter Seven: Going Forth

1. Bhikkhu Ñāṇamoli, *The Life of the Buddha: According to the Pali Canon* (Kandy, Sri Lanka: Buddhist Publication Society, 1972/1992), p. 48.

2. *Ibid.*

3. *Ibid.*, p. 49.

4. Johan Barendregt, "Phobias and Related Fears," trans. Kevin Cook, chapter 13 of *De Zielenmarkt, Over Psychotherapie in Alle Ernst (The Soul-Market, Psychotherapy in All Seriousness)* (Boom: Meppel, 1982), p. 5.

5. *Ibid.*, p. 8.

6. D. W. Winnicott, "Additional Note on Psycho-Somatic Disorder," in *Psycho-Analytic Explorations* (Cambridge, MA: Harvard University Press, 1989), p. 116.

7. *Ibid.*, pp. 116–17.

8. *Ibid.*

9. Michael Eigen, *Eigen in Seoul: Volume One: Madness and Murder* (London: Karnac, 2010), p. 29.

10. D. W. Winnicott, *Playing and Reality* (London and New York: Routledge, 1971), p. 84.

11. Roberto Calasso, *Ka: Stories of the Mind and Gods of India* (New York: Vintage, 1998), p. 280.

12. Robert A. F. Thurman, *Essential Tibetan Buddhism* (New York: HarperCollins, 1996), p. 70.

13. Ñāṇamoli, *Life of the Buddha*, pp. 17–180.

14. Winnicott, *Playing and Reality*, p. 86.

15. Karen Armstrong, *Buddha* (London: Penguin, 2001), p. 66.

16. *Ibid.*
17. *The Voice of the Buddha: The Beauty of Compassion* Volume I, translated by Gwendolyn Bays. (Berkeley, CA: Dharma, 1983), p. 204.
18. Ñāṇamoli, *Life of the Buddha*, p. 21.
19. Sherry Turkle, "The Flight from Conversation," *New York Times*, April 21, 2012.
20. Ñāṇamoli, *Life of the Buddha*, p. 21.
21. *Ibid.*
22. John S. Strong, *The Buddha: A Short Biography* (Oxford: Oneworld, 2001), p. 68.
23. Armstrong, *Buddha*, p. 73.
24. Winnicott, *Playing and Reality*, p. 86.

Chapter Eight: Feelings Matter

1. Richard Gombrich, *What the Buddha Thought* (London: Equinox, 2009), p. 62.
2. *Ibid.*, p. 11.
3. Anālayo, *Satipaṭṭhāna: The Direct Path to Realization* (Cambridge: Windhorse, 2003), p. 164.
4. D. W. Winnicott, *Babies and Their Mothers* (Reading, MA: Addison-Wesley, 1986), p. 86.
5. D. W. Winnicott, "Communicating and Not Communicating Leading to a Study of Certain Opposites," in *The Maturational Processes and the Facilitating Environment* (New York: International Universities Press, 1965), p. 186.
6. Peter Fonagy, *Attachment Theory and Psychoanalysis* (New York: Other Press, 2001), pp. 170–71.

Chapter Nine: Implicit Memory

1. Robert Stolorow, *Trauma and Human Existence: Autobiographical, Psychoanalytic, and Philosophical Reflections* (New York: Routledge, 2007), p. 10.
2. *Ibid.*, p. 20.
3. *Ibid.*
4. Boston Change Process Study Group, "Forms of Relational Meaning: Issues in the Relations Between the Implicit and Reflective-Verbal Domains," *Psychoanalytic Dialogues* 18 (2008): 125–48.
5. *Ibid.*, p. 128.
6. Philip M. Bromberg, *Standing in the Spaces* (Hillsdale, NJ: Analytic Press, 1998), p. 16.
7. D. W. Winnicott, *Playing and Reality* (London and New York: Routledge, 1971), p. 47.
8. *Ibid.*
9. *Ibid.*, p. 81.
10. *Ibid.*, p. 82.
11. *Ibid.*, p. 71.
12. *Ibid.*, p. 65.
13. *Ibid.*, pp. 82–83.
14. Karlen Lyons-Ruth, "The Interface Between Attachment and Intersubjectivity: Perspective from the Longitudinal Study of Disorganized Attachment," *Psychoanalytic Inquiry* 26, no. 4 (2006): 612.
15. D. W. Winnicott, "Fear of Breakdown," in *Psycho-Analytic Explorations* (Cambridge, MA: Harvard University Press, 1989), pp. 90–91.
16. *Ibid.*, p. 92.

Chapter Ten: Dreams of the Buddha

1. Serinity Young, *Dreaming in the Lotus* (Boston: Wisdom, 1999), p. 25.
2. Bhikkhu Ñāṇamoli, *The Life of the Buddha: According to the Pali Canon* (Kandy, Sri Lanka: Buddhist Publication Society, 1972/1992), p. 22.

3. Boston Change Process Study Group, "Forms of Relational Meaning: Issues in the Relations Between the Implicit and Reflective-Verbal Domains," *Psychoanalytic Dialogues* 18 (2008): 125–48.
4. Karlen Lyons-Ruth, "The Interface Between Attachment and Intersubjectivity: Perspective from the Longitudinal Study of Disorganized Attachment," *Psychoanalytic Inquiry* 26, no. 4 (2006): 613.
5. *Ibid.*, p. 602.
6. *Ibid.*, p. 604.
7. Michael Eigen, *Faith and Transformation (Eigen in Seoul, Vol. 2)* (London: Karnac, 2011), p. 20.
8. Bonnie Clearwater, ed., *West Coast Duchamp* (Miami Beach, FL: Grassfield, 1991), p. 107.
9. Philip M. Bromberg, *Awakening the Dreamer* (Mahwah, NJ: Analytic Press, 2006), p. 120.
10. Lyons-Ruth, "Interface Between Attachment and Intersubjectivity," p. 607.
11. *Ibid.*
12. *Ibid.*, p. 608.
13. Jack Kornfield, *A Path with Heart* (New York: Bantam, 1993), p. 28.
14. *Ibid.*
15. *Ibid.*, p. 29.
16. Jeremy Safran, ed., *Psychoanalysis and Buddhism: An Unfolding Dialogue* (Boston: Wisdom, 2003), p. 1.
17. D. W. Winnicott, *Playing and Reality* (London and New York: Routledge, 1971), p. 92.

Chapter Eleven: Reflections of Mind

1. Jack Kornfield, ed., *The Buddha Is Still Teaching: Contemporary Buddhist Wisdom* (Boston & London: Shambhala, 2010), p. 76 (extract entitled "Who is Bothering Whom?" quoting Ajahn Chah).
2. Anālayo, *Satipaṭṭhāna: The Direct Path to Realization* (Cambridge: Windhorse, 2003), p. 3
3. John S. Strong, *The Buddha: A Short Biography* (Oxford: Oneworld, 2001), p. 70.
4. Stephen Batchelor, *Living with the Devil* (New York: Riverhead, 2004), p. 21.
5. Strong, *The Buddha*, p. 71.
6. Batchelor, *Living with the Devil*, p. 19.
7. *Ibid.*, p. 18.
8. *Ibid.*, p. 19.
9. Karen Armstrong, *Buddha* (New York: Penguin, 2001), pp. 90–91.
10. Miranda Shaw, *Buddhist Goddesses of India* (Princeton, NJ: Princeton University Press, 2006), p. 21.
11. Bhikkhu Ñāṇamoli, *The Life of the Buddha: According to the Pali Canon* (Kandy, Sri Lanka: Buddhist Publication Society, 1972/1992), p. 27.
12. *The Voice of the Buddha, The Beauty of Compassion*, Volume II, translated by Gwendolyn Bays, (Berkeley: Dharma, 1983), p. 482.
13. Shaw, *Buddhist Goddesses of India*, p. 20.
14. *Ibid.*, p. 25.
15. Strong, *The Buddha*, p. 72.
16. Batchelor, *Living with the Devil*, p. 6.
17. Robert Stolorow, *Trauma and Human Existence: Autobiographical, Psychoanalytic, and Philosophical Reflections* (New York: Routledge, 2007), p. 20.
18. *Ibid.*
19. *Ibid.*, p. 16.
20. Sherab Chödzin Kohn, *A Life of the Buddha* (Boston: Shambhala, 2009), pp. 32–33.
21. Batchelor, *Living with the Devil*, p. 10.
22. Lucien Stryk, *World of the Buddha* (New York: Grove Weidenfeld, 1968), p. 271.
23. Robert Thurman, *Essential Tibetan Buddhism* (New York: HarperSanFrancisco, 1995), p. 99.

Chapter Twelve: A Relational Home

1. Robert Stolorow, *Trauma and Human Existence: Autobiographical, Psychoanalytic, and Philosophical Reflections* (New York, Routledge, 2007), p .10.
2. Personal communication; See Joseph LeDoux, *The Emotional Brain: The Mysterious Underpinnings of Emotional Life* (New York: Simon & Schuster, 1996). See also Joseph LeDoux, Lizabeth Romanski, and Andrew Xagoraris, "Indelibility of Subcortical Emotional Memories," *Journal of Cognitive Neuroscience*, vol. 1 (July 1989): 238–43.
3. Adam Phillips, *Missing Out: In Praise of the Unlived Life* (London: Hamish Hamilton, 2012), p. 35.
4. *Ibid.*
5. Helen Davey, "Wounded but Resilient: The Impact of Trauma," *Psychology Today*, October 30, 2011.
6. *Ibid.*
7. Robert Thurman, *Essential Tibetan Buddhism* (San Francisco: Harper San Francisco, 1995), pp. 209–10.
8. Storolowe, *Trauma and Human Existence*, p. 16.
9. *The Blue Cliff Record*, translated by Thomas Cleary and J.C. Cleary (Boston and London: Shambhala, 2005), p. 176.
10. Stephen Batchelor, *Living with the Devil* (New York: Riverhead, 2004), p. 55.
11. *Ibid.*, p. 574.
12. Adam Phillips, *Winnicott* (Cambridge, MA: Harvard University Press, 1988), p. 29.

Index